Makers of Fire

The Spirituality of Leading From the Future

Alex McManus

IMN Idea Lab
USA
SA
UK

Makers of Fire: the spirituality of leading from the future
© 2014 by Alex McManus

Published by IMN Idea Lab

For more information about the International Mentoring Network, visit our main site at http://theimn.com. (Be sure to subscribe to our newsletter!) Follow the IMN's twitter at @theimn.

To follow Alex McManus, check out his Website at alexmcmanus.org, Twitter at @alex_mcmanus, Instagram at http://instagram.com/xandermcmanus, and Facebook at https://www.facebook.com/alexmcmanus.

ADDITIONAL TRAINING AND RESOURCES
The IMN offers training for leaders interested in developing their strategic foresight, creativity, and spiritual leadership. See our website for more information - http://theimn.com

Dedication

Niza, Yes, the robots may soon revolt. In any case,
I'll have dinner ready when you get home. Always.

Mom, As a teenager you took a chance and began
a globetrotting adventure that would create a better
future for so many of us.

Michael, my first son.
You see things few others do. Thanks for what you teach me.
Erica, my sole daughter.
If I could name you all over again, I'd call you Unique.
Lucas, my youngest son.
The whole world is open to you. Swing away.
Natalie and Jake, So very glad we've become family.

To my brother, Erwin, a Maker of Fire, and his family, Kim, Aaron, Mariah, and Patty.

The IMN network pioneers, my tribe of fire makers. Boom!

CONTENTS

Introduction   6

She - Vision   11

Section 1: Fuel   14

Tattooing the Earth   15

The Only Real Miracle 20

To Make All Things Thrive 28

The Anthropocene   33

Undercurrents   44

Artifacts   56

Scouting the Futures 60

Weak Signals   66

Mysterious Behavior 69

Kinds of Futures   77

Smoke on the Horizon 81

Trajectories   85

Describing the Present 90

She - Incubation   97

Section 2: Oxygen   99

Drowning   100

The First Futurist   104

Once Upon a Time   109

Blue Moments   120

The Air We Breathe   127

What Does it Mean

to be Human?   131

She - Flickers   144

Section 3: Heat   146

Sparks   147

Incoming Firestorms   157

The Fire Makers   163

Burn   181

Abraham in Space   185

Postscript: The After Party   188

She - Hackers of the Universe   198

More IMN Resources   200

Introduction
The Art of Making Fire

In the beginning the world was dark. The first humans moved at night by whatever light the moon might offer. Half of their day was governed by sunlight. And the other half by dread.

Then came the change.

Somewhere in the fog of prehistory, humankind lit up the night. In one of our most distinguishing achievements, we domesticated wild fire. Until then we were naked primates, fangless and thin-skinned, scavenging on the margins of the Pleistocene era. Harnessing the power of fire was our breakthrough technology, the first step on a journey that began with overcoming the night and led to ruling the world.

The Triad of Fire

For fire to happen, three ingredients must combine:

> **fuel**, material that fire consumes;

> **oxygen**, the flow of air that coaxes fire to life; and

> **heat** to ignite the process.

These three ingredients make up the "Triangle of Combustion."

Fuel + Oxygen + Heat = Fire

The Triangle of Combustion creates the base for my analogy. This Triad of Fire answers the question, How does the burning event called *fire* happen?

Corresponding to the Triad of Fire, the Triad of Change has three ingredients.

Artifacts. The Fuel of change is made up of the stuff we create, man-made Artifacts. The artifacts of our time include issues, trends, technologies, social structures, and events.

Meaning. The nurturing flow of Oxygen which leads to change is the Meaning we attribute to the world around us. It is the common substance of purpose, belief, trust, and hope.

Creativity. The Heat which kindles change is human choice. It is the spark of Creativity, the ignition of leadership, the flashpoint of imagination manifested in action.

Fuel + Oxygen + Heat = Fire
Artifacts + Meaning + Creativity = Change

The Triad of Change answers the question, How does social change come about?

Social change happens when the Heat of human Creativity engages the Fuel, the Artifacts (relevant issues, trends, social practices, thinking, and events) of the moment, and nurtures it with Oxygen, a Meaning and purpose that captures the imagination.

Corresponding to the Triads of Fire and Change, the Triad of Leadership has three ingredients.

Describe. Leading from the future requires the courage to fearlessly *describe* the present. Leaders must stare down the disruptive specter of exponential change across the domains of society, technology, economics, environment, and politics and fearlessly state what they see.

Discern Leading from the future requires the insight to wisely *discern* meaning within the mix of current reality. Leaders must dare to highlight what from our past we need to sustain, what we need to let go, and what we need to create.

Discover. Leading from the future requires the innovation to *discover* creative paths towards a better future. Leaders inspire others to work together for a world that works for everyone.

Fuel + Oxygen + Heat = Fire
Artifacts + Meaning + Creativity = Change
Describe + Discern + Discover = Leadership

This third triad, the Triad of Leadership, answers the question, What is the leadership task in times of rapid change like ours?

Like the fire makers of old, we are again on the threshold of great breakthroughs.

The fields of genetics and nanotechnology may create a new kind of humanity and the "Jurassic Park" style resurrection of extinct species.

Studies in human rejuvenation seek to escape the gravitic pull of aging and death.

Our burgeoning electronic networks may one day awaken in some form of artificial intelligence.

Robots, once common only in our factories, will soon be common in our daily lives: traveling about our neighborhoods, living in our homes, working at our local grocery stores.

The discovery of many Earth-like planets may lead to the discovery of extraterrestrial life.

The privatization of the space industry may lead to the first human colonies on Mars.

In the next hundred years, we will initiate and experience more change than in our first two million, and we will touch the lives of generations not yet born.

At this point in our history, with our expanding technological capacities, we must engage a new dimension of the human imagination. We must lead from the future.

And you? Where do you fit in all of this?

You are the maker of fire.

SHE

She stretched like a young lioness and inhaled deeply. Even at this distance she could taste the smoke in the morning air. For as long as she could remember, fifteen dry seasons, she'd been following the fires with her clan. Every year when the smoke appeared on the horizon, the clan would migrate towards the burning rim and camp so close you could hear the crackling fire as it consumed the earth. From there they would wait for the predatory flames to drive frantic prey directly into their pointed sticks.

Fire, as voracious and unpredictable as it was, made for a perfect partner.

Once, when almost starved from days of an unfruitful hunt, they found an animal that had been roasted alive. Until then they'd never approached the blackened bodies of animals charred by fire. But in their hunger they dragged it from the ashes and discovered that parts of the burned carcass were especially tender.

From this they'd learned to use the fires to soften their kill when they could. The meat was better, easier to chew, and kept longer. As far as the clan was concerned, fire was their friend and ally.

The hunting party set out before the sunrise and traveled far along the rim of fire in search of prey. She trailed behind the party, pondering a vision. For two fire seasons now, every time she'd come across an animal in the ash, she'd seen in her mind's eye a smoldering coal within an upside down skull. Sometimes her visions were so vivid that she'd squeeze her eyes in unbelief and look again. Upon closer examination, the skulls were always empty.

She squatted near another skull now, pondering the vision, and trying to hear what, if anything, the fires were saying. Fire had chased this antelope into a thorn-tree thicket where it must have been entangled, and antelope and thicket alike had been devoured. Thornwood burned long and hot, well after grasses had cooled to ash, but it had done so before her clan had come along, so there was nothing useful left of either fire or meat. Only skull and bones among smoldering roots.

She dug her pointed stick beneath the embers around the skull, lifted a live coal above the parched ground, and placed it on a clump of dry grass. She stood and turned to face the warm golden light of the rising sun. A soft breeze passed and her long and frayed mane flowed behind her. At her feet, the dry grass burst into flame.

"We are fire creatures from an ice age."

Fire, Stephen Pyne

FUEL

Chapter 1

Tattooing the Earth

Even though there were lion in the area, I knew I was safe in our enclosed camp. Still, the night was so dark that I stopped in my tracks wondering if I should follow my instinctive fear and retrace my steps or if I should follow my sense of direction and proceed forward. Based on my mental map of our camp, I knew my destination should lie through the tall golden grass directly ahead of me.

The wind passed by and the grass seemed to whisper, taunting what I thought I knew. I stood perfectly still in the dark, all my senses engaged. Inconveniently, I remembered a conversation from earlier that day: If a lion were stalking you, I was told, you wouldn't even know it.

Even in my perfectly safe context, how I wanted light.

Orbital photos of the Earth's nightside sparkle with city lights. But in the beginning it was dark. So, so dark. Imagine orbiting the Earth a thousand years ago, before the Saracens developed street lighting, or some two million years ago, before man tamed fire. These views of the Earth at night would be significantly different from the views of Earth we see today. That was the world *before* man captured fire.

The Birth of Fire

Fire expert Stephen Pyne calls the three ingredients of fire (fuel, oxygen, and heat) the "Combustion Triangle." All three ingredients must be present to catalyze the event called fire. Somewhere around four hundred million years ago, all three existed in sufficient quantity and the Earth was visited and colonized by "First Fires."

First Fires erupt by the interaction of natural elements. A spark [the heat of ignition] caused by a strike of lightning, the impact of a meteor, or perhaps a blistering volcanic flow, met with organic material [fuel] in dry-enough conditions. This meeting of the heat of ignition and fuel was nurtured by free flowing air [oxygen]; and fire, First Fire, was born.

Millions of years would pass before the "Second Fires" would come. Somewhere, perhaps in the savannas of east Africa, and somewhen, perhaps in the neighborhood of two million years ago, ancient humans became the spark. Prehistoric people of vision, invention, and motivation stepped between the elements of oxygen and fuel with the heat of ignition, and Second Fire, anthropogenic fire, fire originated by humans, was born.

These original Makers of Fire stood in the mystic reality between two worlds.

The first world was a dark and cold world where fire was useful but capricious. Early humans may have followed the signs of wild fire and used it as a natural ally in the hunt. If fortunate, they may have also at times feasted on the roasted meat of animals killed in the blaze. But fire came only when the gods sent it, and without warning.

The second world, after we learned to make fire at will, was brighter, warmer, and safer.

I've often wondered how this transition from one world to the next happened. How did ancient peoples discover the secrets of making fire? Was this discovery made by one person at one time and place? Was it then spread from there to others? Or, was the alchemy of fire-making discovered at many times and places by many people?

Perhaps it all began by tending captured fire. The early humans may have learned to gather coals from wild fire. Eventually they learned to feed the coals the fuel of dry organic materials. Over time they learned through observation that fire thrives when nurtured by air. If successful in sustaining the fire's life, they may have carted the fire around like a deity in their midst. They would seek to extend the life of their fire as long as possible. Different clans may have had fire of differing ages. Some tribal fires may have been new but others may have had a life span of years. But, if their fire ever went out, they would be dependent on that random strike of lightning, that bolt from the gods, for the initial energy of ignition.

The next step was a quantum leap. Perhaps a persistent person of vision and innovation was visited by a game-changing idea. What that idea was — striking stone upon stone to release a brief hot spark, or spinning a stick into a nest of tinder to bring it to combustion —and how they came upon it, we'll never know. But somehow they stepped into the triangle of combustion, between fuel and oxygen, and provided the heat of ignition. When they did, the making of fire was no longer the exclusive domain of the gods of chance.

They gave birth to the Second Fires and ignited a new future for humanity, one that may not have existed without them. In other words, in that instant when they changed their world they created the pathways to ours.

Second Fire became the first layer of what Kevin Kelly, one of the founders of Wired Magazine, coined the "Technium," a world in which layers upon layers of interconnected technologies developed over two million years and formed a kind of living exoskeleton around the human species. But in the early days of Second

Fire, it was a singular work of magic. In the old world, humans followed fire. In this new world, fire lived among men.

I imagine that first generation of fire makers would gather their children around their fire and tell stories of the world *before* fire came to live among humans. They would tell the story of how the woman gave birth to fire, changing their world so much and so quickly. The old world, the one in which fire was rare, capricious, and wild, was an indelible personal experience for that first generation, but stories about the dark times must have seemed like fables to her children and grandchildren. The post-fire generations, as they built upon the breakthrough technology of domesticated fire, would increasingly lose touch with the cold and dark world their parents and grandparents knew.

*****

Ancient humans must have been a scrappy lot. Unlike birds of prey with their visual acuity, speed, and sharp talons, and unlike great felines with their powerful bulk and sharp daggers for teeth, pre-fire humans had only sticks for digging and hitting, rocks for scraping and grinding, stones for throwing. No fangs or talons to speak of, no armored hide, no wings to fly nor claws to burrow quickly into the sand. Without the physical endowments given to other animals, especially predators, humans before mastering fire must have been marginalized, vulnerable, scavenging creatures.

After mastering fire, we were like gods.

Some say that we became human when we domesticated fire. According to myth, Prometheus stole fire from the gods and gave it to humans. With the seemingly supernatural gift of creating fire at will, the age of human ascendance was born, and humans began to change the Earth.

In fact, the presence of a layer of coal, a hearth, and charred bones are signs that prehistoric humans had once occupied a site. If fire were a living thing, we would say the relationship was symbiotic: humans took care of fire and fire helped man survive and thrive. Together, man and fire would tattoo the Earth in the geological layer informally called the Anthropocene, the Era of Man. Their creativity changed the shape of their societies and the course of future history.

What they did touched us.

*****

As I stood perfectly still in the whispering golden grass of a South African field, trying to decide on the best path back to my cabin, I quieted my breathing only to hear my heart pounding. Defining reality is not always easy. And you can only say *There is no lion* to yourself so many times. Eventually you have to choose a path. What I would have given to see any kind of light… a flash light, a kitchen light, a torch light, a candlelight, an outdoor lamp lighting the way back to my cabin. What I would have given for any sign of Second Fire.

Chapter 2

The Only Real Miracle

Faith, like fire, doesn't dispel the darkness. It creates a space within it. Faith creates a womb for hope and love within a universe that seems indifferent to both.

The character, Homer Simpson, of the animated series the Simpsons, once visited with Ned, the "God dude," while high on medical marijuana. He tells Ned he has a question for him, pulls out a piece of paper, and asks, "Could Jesus microwave a burrito so hot that he himself could not eat it?"

Faith lives with paradox.

The first line of the Bible: "When God began, he created the heavens and the earth..." establishes the premise of faith. If one accepts the Creator God as the premise, the events, even the miraculous ones, that follow in the story fall in place.

And yet, I think there is in reality only one true miracle, and we have yet to see it. At best, we've seen it only once.

*****

The first chapter of Genesis is a poem of creation which crescendos in the creation of the humankind. Chapter two of Genesis introduces the Garden of Eden and Adam and Eve, representatives of the first humans.

Genesis chapter three describes what has come to be known by many as the "fall" of man through which God's perfect creation becomes the imperfect world as we know it.

The Genesis stories of creation and flood were adapted and woven together from ancient stories about human origins, pain, suffering, and disasters, and were eventually tied to the history of a particular people.

This vision of primordial humans in a garden may be just as much a dream of an ideal human future as it is a vision of an idyllic past. I consider these "first" humans as poetic figures. They are placeholders that explain the history of human experience but they are also anticipations of what we can become in futurity. In other words, the human story still waits for the first humans. I touch on this idea again later in the book. Either way these stories are an indication that, from the perspective of the writers, we are not (yet) what God intended.

The human story starts in the Garden of Eden, the world as these early humans imagined it could be. The main characters are Adam and Eve who together represent humankind. God trusts them with everything in His garden. He permits them everything except the fruit of one tree.

It's a well known story to most of you. Adam and Eve betray God's trust and eat the forbidden fruit. Because of this betrayal, the first humans are expelled from the Garden and find themselves in the weeds outside.

It's there, outside the garden, in the land east of Eden, that the writers introduce two brothers, the sons of Adam and Eve, named Cain and Abel (Genesis chapter 4). We are about to learn that Adam and Eve's betrayal is not an isolated event. It's the beginning of a descent.

What happens between Cain and Abel immortalizes them. Ask almost anyone in the western world, and they will have some inkling of these two brothers.

As the story unfolds, in ancient fashion, Cain and Abel bring offerings to the Lord. God accepts Abel's but isn't pleased with Cain's, and a change comes over Cain.

"Then the Lord said to Cain, 'Why are you so angry? Why is your face downcast?'" (Genesis 4.6)

This dialogue anticipates one of the most brutal acts in all of literature. Even if we don't understand why God accepts one offering but not the other, we fully understand the danger of the moment. We know that jealousy, resentment, and anger can violently possess our kind.

And, even though God is trying to help Cain, we also know that reason alone does not change the will. We've seen it before when we've tried to help someone set on a ruinous course. That person who is fighting demon-like addictions, or devoured by lust, or obsessed by the need for a thrill, cannot be saved by reason alone.

But God tries anyway, just like we do.

The God character here is not an indifferent force that doesn't care what happens. His creation has gone wrong but he stays engaged. Why he doesn't simply undo what he's created and start again, we won't know until much, much later in the story.

What God does do is try to influence the human.

"Then the Lord said to Cain... 'If you do what is right, will you not be accepted?'" (Genesis 4.6-7)

Do what's right, God tells Cain, and you'll feel better. He then warns Cain about the danger of the moment.

"But if you do not do what is right, sin is crouching at your door; it desires to have you, but you must rule over it." (Genesis 4.6-7)

God makes Cain aware of the present. Cain has choices. He warns him of the near future, of the peril of choosing unwisely. In other words, God paints for Cain a picture of alternative futures. The first is one in which Abel lives and Cain avoids the demons waiting to possess him. The second is one in which Abel dies and Cain becomes a slave to an evil passenger.

*****

Many believe that Cain did not really have a choice. The first humans, Adam and Eve, took his freedom away with their original betrayal. Sin had already pounced on them all and they were all enslaved by evil.

Some read this text through the filter of a sovereign God who knows the future and thus predetermines everything. Cain has no freedom to choose. God and God alone creates the future. God cannot be dependent on the man.

But we must also ask, Is God's offer to Cain real? Is Cain's future really open? Does he really have the power to pivot in the moment? Can he create one future by choosing one path and a different future by choosing another? Does God really invite Cain to create a future together with him? Does God really leave himself vulnerable to the possibility that Cain might diverge and desire a future of his own design? Didn't God already try this with Adam and Eve?

The story suggests at this intersection a creative seam in the fabric of reality.

A natural reading suggests that God isn't pretending. History may be closed to human input, but futurity is open. God isn't offering an unavailable possibility.

At this moment in the story we know that there is no such thing as *the* future. There are only the *futures*, plural. Reality exists in at least two layers: actuality, and multiple possibilities.

Cain stands at a fork in his journey.

Now, in the world of the biblical story, in Cain's field of vision, the blur between two alternative futures snaps into focus. In the first future there exists a brother named Abel. In the second future, there is no Abel.

Paradoxically, Cain has no choice but to choose.

If he wants, Cain can choose a human path. God warns him: if you choose poorly, sin is lurking to pounce on you. What path will Cain embrace? How will he exercise his extraordinary powers?

"Now Cain said to his brother Abel, 'Let's go out to the field.' While they were in the field, Cain attacked his brother Abel and killed him." (Genesis 4.8)

Like all of us, Cain entered the human story in the middle of the telling. He lived in a world already tainted with evil. We too experience the reality of evil. Cain lived in a world of betrayal and hurt. We too experience relational disconnection. Cain is marked by the past exile of his family from the Garden of Eden. We too are shaped by our past.

Like Cain, we too can shape the futures. In times past, our decisions impacted those around us in the near term. But today, our decisions can impact the world and those who live upon it for thousands of years. Like Cain, we must learn to navigate the future better. Unlike Cain, we can destroy the world. We must learn to think more long term. Our choices can shape not only our tomorrows… but the millennia.

*****

As Abel's life soaked the earth, Cain awakened a world less than human. Stepping out of the biblical narrative for a moment, there must have been a time in the evolution of our species when there was not yet a word for murder or for war. Humans created new words to name new things. This was new.

In the wake of the first murder, God asks Cain,

"Where is your brother Abel?"

"I don't know," Cain replied. "Am I my brother's keeper?" (Genesis 4.9)

The rest of the biblical story is an attempt to answer Cain's question.

Following Cain's denial of responsibility for his brother's welfare, God confronts Cain about the future he created:

"The Lord said, 'What have you done? Listen! Your brother's blood cries out to me from the ground. Now you are under a curse and driven from the ground, which opened its mouth to receive your brother's blood from your hand. When you work the ground, it will no longer yield its crops for you. You will be a restless wanderer on the earth.'" (Genesis 4.10-12)

From chapter three and the "fall of man" and --in the space of only three chapters-- by Genesis chapter six, we have traveled far from Eden, and the descent into darkness is near complete:

"The Lord saw how great the wickedness of the human race had become on earth, and that every inclination of the thoughts of the human heart was only evil

all of the time. The Lord regretted that he had made human beings on the earth, and his heart was deeply troubled." (Genesis 6.5-6)

In the total space of six chapters we move from a world in which God admires every aspect of his creation saying, *"It is very good,"* to one in which God *"regrets"* that he made humankind. God does not regret making the mosquito, pesky as it is. But man breaks his heart.

*****

While the writers of Genesis exhibited hope, they had a realistic view of human nature. They saw that the human heart conjures up and intends evil. They also had an insight into a mysterious principle at work in our lives. Every person, like Cain, is free to choose against evil, even though wrapped in a context tainted by it. Yet, people seem to consistently choose unwisely.

Why?

Eventually even God himself shakes his head with disbelief.

Like a virus, this mysterious passenger infects us all. While most of us never manifest its most devastating symptoms, we all carry it.

This story suggests something else surprising. God is powerless.

To fix the situation with Cain, God can erase his creation. He can set the heavens and the earth on fire. He can destroy Cain and every other human. He can set loose from the deep the dragons of chaos and allow them to devour the cosmos.

But rather than erupt in power he remains in a posture of powerlessness. Sure, he can stop Cain from killing Abel. But he can't force Cain to love him. Love must be freely given. Power is useless in matters of love.

And this suggests what may be the only real miracle.

If God can create everything that exists, then he can tweak it. Miracles are not that hard to fathom given the premise of a Creator God. If he has the power, shall we say, the technology, to create the oceans, then he can certainly part the seas. If he has the technologies to create life, then he can certainly raise the dead. These are not really that amazing when you consider the premise.

But how will God create a future inhabited by truly good creatures? How can he shape a future in which women and men with the power of choice, like Cain, choose always to do the right thing, the good thing, the beautiful thing without eliminating their freedom to choose? How can God inspire perfect love?

That would truly be a miracle.

Chapter 3

To Make All Things Thrive

According to Genesis, God has made man like himself: creative. If the Earth is characterized by an amazing diversity of life all unfolding from a common source in a dynamic ebb and flow from era to era, the Anthropocene is characterized by the creative impact of the human.

Creativity is a clue that we are not locked into a purely predetermined system of cause and effect. While all human choice is preceded by causes and followed by effects, and the menu of choices may be limited, creativity suggests room for novelty and surprise.

Sometimes a cause may provoke a novel effect. There may occasionally be, in contrast to Solomon's lament, something new under the sun.

The first line of Genesis chapter one is a dependent clause, *"When God began to create the heavens and the earth..."* How many times God has created we are not told. He may be a seasoned creator or he may be a novice experiencing the act of creation for the first time.

The dependent clause is followed by a dynamic parenthetical phrase, *"...the earth was formless and void and the spirit of God vibrated over the face of the deep..."* A case can be made that God does not, according to these lines of verse, create *ex nihilo* - out of nothing. Rather, like an artist in a studio, he creates from raw materials.

In this reading, the story of God begins where all good stories begin, in the middle.

Finally, we arrive at the independent clause towards which these words are driving, *"He said, 'Let there be light.'"* (Genesis 1.1-3)

As God begins to create, he turns on the lights.

God began creating and then passed the baton to the creation itself. He delegated to the land the production of vegetation:

"Then God said, "Let the land produce vegetation: seed-bearing plants and trees on the land that bear fruit with seed in it, according to their various kinds." (Genesis 1.11)

To the water and the sky he delegated the creatures of the sea and air: *"Let the water teem with living creatures, and let birds fly above the earth across the vault of the sky."* In the same line the poets attribute the creation of the sea creatures to God: *"So God created the great creatures of the sea and every living thing with which the water teems and that moves about in it, according to their kinds, and every winged bird according to its kind."* (Genesis 1.20-21)

In the view of the genesis poem, our world of living things regenerates itself as an act of God. The land, the water, and the skies are a canvas on which living things co-create with God. The Creator and the creatures are at once and the same time partners in the creation. The discoverable mechanics of the natural world, the evolution of life, are all fingerprints of God at work.

The Creator then surveys his work:

"And God saw that it was good. God blessed them and said, 'Be fruitful and increase in number and fill the water in the seas, and let the birds increase on the earth.'" (Genesis 1.22)

And finally the poets tell us that God made humans.

"Let us make mankind in our image, in our likeness, so that they may rule over the fish in the sea and the birds in the sky, over the livestock and all the wild animals, and over all the creatures that move along the ground."

So God created mankind in his own image,

in the image of God he created them;

male and female he created them.

God blessed them and said to them, "Be fruitful and increase in number; fill the earth and subdue it. Rule over the fish in the sea and the birds in the sky and over every living creature that moves on the ground." (Genesis 1.26-28)

The writers conclude the creation poem, "*God saw all that he had made, and it was very good.*" (Genesis 1.31)

And we, along with the other creatures, continued the creative work. And the biosphere continued to blossom, to open like the petals of a flower revealing layer after layer of beauty.

According to Genesis chapter 1, God is at work when life thrives.

And what is the role of humankind? Humans are designed to represent God within creation. They are equipped and commissioned to make all things thrive.

Some don't like the idea of humans "ruling over" the Earth. I think it's because we've seen how humans rule over things, and we don't like it.

Genesis chapter one shows what happens when God rules. Life bursts open the seams and thrives. Thriving is the metric by which human rulership can be measured.

*****

The writers of Genesis, in seeking to describe their world, also described what the world could be. This vision raises questions. Why does a creature designed to be the guardian of life become a master of war? How can we move from where we are now to where we want to be?

While the desire to change the world may reflect the naiveté of youth, leading from the future must inspire each person to believe that a more human future is possible.

What does it mean to lead *from* the future? It means developing a picture of the future one prefers in the context of the alternative futures that are possible, cultivating the action-mindset to create the preferred future, and calling on others to join you.

Many of us lead from the past, that is, we do what's always been done the way it's been done. We simply repeat the past in a never ending circle. It's like being stuck in a hamster's wheel.

All organizations are vulnerable to this (not just conservative ones). Leading from the future means getting out of the wheel and forging a new way forward. Ultimately, every vision must carry within it the image of a world that works for everyone. This "world that works" doesn't exist anywhere except in the imagination.

So, a part of leading from the future is to feed the imagination.

Feeding the imagination a compelling vision touches the hearth of the human heart, the place where dreams are born. And dreams are the DNA of new futures.

The information within our dreams has yet to fully blossom into the future we want. That future will not be made real by analysis, reason or big data. These look too much at the world as it is. This matters. It's important to be able to describe and define reality. But they aren't enough.

For us to thrive will require more than big data. It will require courage. New paths will be carved in the wilds of the future by those moved by faith, hope, and love. For these look at both what the world is (describing reality) and what it could become (discerning meaning).

The *spirituality* of leading from the future isn't about eschatology, the biblical doctrine of "the last things." It's about futurity, the imagining of possible, probable, and preferred futures in order to make transformative changes of direction in the present.

This spirituality isn't an acquired taste or an add-on capability. It sits at the core of what we can become as a species. It's based on our ability to describe reality, to see the data, the world as it is, and our capacity to dream, to imagine the world as it could be, to discern meaning.

Like Cain we have no choice but to choose. In other words, we are creative. Like Cain we have no option but to be responsible for our choices. In other words, we are spiritual.

*****

When Cain asked God, am I my brother's keeper? It's obvious that the answer is a resounding "No!"

Cain was not his brother's keeper. He was far more than that.

He was his brother's brother.

In other words, to thrive we'll need to remember who we are. We can't thrive alone. We can only thrive together.

In the 21st century, humans must turn towards a spirituality of thriving. Data may tell us what we need to know in order to survive. But spirituality and creativity tell us what we need to thrive. Thriving is where the impetus to survive meets both the craving for beauty and the need to love.

We are the guardians of Earth and of each other. It's our responsibility to ensure both thrive.

Chapter 4

The Anthropocene

What drives change? Change comes from at least three driving forces:

- trends
- events
- human choice

The TED (Technology, Entertainment, and Design) conference ran a survey at their Vancouver 2014 gathering. The topic was "Change" and the participants were asked, "What will be the most significant drivers of change over the next 30 years?" They listed ten options on their survey and each option was accompanied by a quote from a leading advocate for that "driver" of change. The options were:

Climate Crisis

"Our world faces a true planetary emergency." — Al Gore

Rising Inequality

"To be sure that this new economy benefits us all and not just the plutocrats, we need a new New Deal." — Chrystia Freeland

Aging Populations

"My father, 92, says: 'Let's stop talking only about how to save the old folks and start talking about how to get them to save us all.'" — Laura Carstensen

Online Learning

"What happens when every precocious 13-year-old in the world has access to every bit of information they could ever want?" — Salman Khan

Transparency v. Privacy

Just as the Internet has opened up the world for each and every one of us, it has also opened up each and every one of us to the world. — Gary Kovacs

Space Technology

"Do we want to be a space-faring civilization exploring the stars ... or forever confined to Earth until some eventual extinction event?" — Elon Musk

Machine Intelligence

"By the 2030s, the nonbiological portion of our intelligence will predominate." — Ray Kurzweil

Work Reinvented

"The key to winning the race isn't to compete against machines but to compete with machines." — Erik Brynjolfsson and Andrew McAfee

Genomics Revolution

"I firmly believe that the next great breakthrough in bioscience could come from a 15-year-old who downloads the human genome in Egypt." — Thomas Friedman

Internet of Things

"This is like the birth of the Internet, but it's literally an Internet of things. It's an Internet where data becomes things and things become data." — Neil Gershenfeld

I'm certain that we who create such lists as TED's are cognizant that humans drive change. And stating "humans!" within each item on a list would be unnecessarily cumbersome.

But some of us feel powerless. We feel helpless against the impersonal forces of "the machine," or the government, or religion, or the corporation, or the union, or the masses, or big data, or technology.

We need to be reminded: humans are powerful drivers of change. And, as importantly, you as an individual have a unique power, the power to choose, to create, to influence, to shape.

Human creativity drives change and it serves us, from time to time, to make this explicit.

When I speak of change, I mean ideas, words, and/or deeds that make the future course of human relationships different from what they have been, are, or would be if left alone. When I speak of creativity, I mean the human capacity to make or do things that others value.

In the TED list above, former vice-president Al Gore talks about a "planetary emergency" in the form of a "climate crisis" and Elon Musk, founder of Tesla and space entrepreneur (SpaceX), talks about a "space-faring civilization."

The sense of scale here is accurate: the changes that must happen among us are epic.

While I am a believer that humanity must reach for the stars, the greatest challenge before us isn't the quest to make humanity a multi-planetary species. The greatest challenge is the quest to make humanity human. This will require more than knowledge. It will require wisdom.

In this quest many of the greatest battles will be fought in the everyday lives of overly plump 21st century *homo sapiens*. Indeed, it may prove easier to colonize another planet than to make humanity a species worth exporting across the galaxy.

Elon Musk believes it's possible to set humans on Mars by 2026. India has just placed a satellite in orbit around the Red Planet. The Mars One project is already taking applications for a potential colony.

Now that the era of private enterprise in space is here, we may soon become a multi-planetary species. But as important as traveling to the stars will be, we must also journey far on our adventure of becoming human. A more human future will not be handed down to us from the centralized empires of power that are emerging. We'll have to create that future at the heart level. That's why everyone, not just politicians and venture capitalists, must prepare to lead from the future.

*****

When we think about what drives change, many of us automatically think of technology. The TED list is full of technology driven change. As I stood in the tall grass of our South African camp that night, I felt a shiver as I imagined the vulnerability of living in the wild, naked of technology. We are naked no longer.

The metaphor of Makers of Fire grants technology a huge role in driving change. Twenty-first century humans are wrapped in layer upon layer of technology. We travel in it, live in it, sit on it, eat with it, brush our teeth with it, wake up with it, work and socialize with it, learn and think by it, keep alert by it, talk to it, go to sleep by it.

We build massive human hives called cities, burrow underneath the earth with subways and mines, and mark the earth with intricate webs we call highways and railways. Our ocean floors are laced with cables and pipelines and their surfaces mottled with plastics like the Pacific Garbage Gyre.

In the not-too-distant future, robots will begin taking human jobs in places like the shopping mall, fast food restaurants, and construction sites, thus creating another layer between us and labor. UAVs (Unmanned Aerial Vehicles, that is, flying robots) are already flying in our commercial airspace. Our clothes will become a kind of human barcode tracking our every move and activity. The merger of fashion with technology will make everything we wear a form of biotelemetry that tracks everything from our whereabouts to our vital signs.

Eventually, our minds may wirelessly interface with the ubiquitous ocean of information in which we will live. Our smart homes will take over our household maintenance chores for us, keeping track of what we need, and alerting us when those items are available at the store on sale. The items we need could then be robotically delivered or printed by our 3D printers.

Ever since humans domesticated fire, technology has been a driver of social change. We may even feel superior to those long-forgotten primitives who first made fire. But what would happen to us if we suddenly found ourselves in the wilds with nothing but the resources available to ancient man? Would we even know how to begin to start a fire?

We turn on lights, plug in appliances, and start the engines of our automobiles without any sense of how they work. We are removed from the process and are simply end-users that operate the technology.

But humans are not (yet) extensions of technology. Technology is still an extension of man. Medicine is an extension of our desire to heal, weapons of our desire to hurt, mobile devices of our desire to stay connected. As important as technology is as a driver of change, we must not dismiss the central importance of human agency in igniting and shaping the world. Technology is the hands of man.

*****

Others, like Al Gore, think of the environment as a major driver of social change. Though many environmentally-minded people suffer the hallmark of bad thinking — the inability to objectively see and weigh the benefits of industrialization along with the costs, to factor in the good of fossil fuels along with the bad — responsibility to make the world thrive is a part of the Genesis vision for humanity. Environmentalists remind us that the natural world can be a fragile as well as a powerful driver of change. From gradual climate change that causes superstorms, droughts and famines, to sudden climate change caused by asteroid impacts, natural events can and do drive change.

When it comes the future of the environment, we must identify two opposing philosophical points of view among us. On the one hand, some believe that the goal of our work should be to harness natural resources to maximize human well-being. This high view of people is a huge positive. The negative can be an unsustainable and consumeristic waste of our resources. On the other hand, others feel that the goal of our work should be to minimize the human impact on our planet. The positive here is a rich view of our ecosystems and a concern, even love, for all of life. The negative here is a self-hatred, a hatred of the human race.

*****

38

In Classical thought, fire — certainly an important environmental force of change — is one of four elements that constitute the essential components of reality. The others are Earth, Water, and Air. Of these four only fire is an event, not a substance.

Render them all as events and you might have Quake, Flood, Hurricane, and Fire. While we can now create fire, we cannot yet spin a tornado, turn a tide, or cause a temblor.

But our responses to and initiatives within the environment have become weighty. Against the cold and dangers of night, we created fire. Built shelter. Harnessed electricity. Invented light.

The spaces we designed made winters as warm as the tropics and the night light up like day. We split the atom and created a heat so sinister that entire cities burned to a crisp.

We have ourselves become a force of nature. There is now Quake, Flood, Hurricane, Fire, and Creativity. That's why, as critical as our environmental issues are, the greatest planetary emergency before us isn't the environment. It is human evil. It is us.

Still, when it comes to drivers of change, we rarely list "human creativity." Perhaps it's because we tend to think of humans as perceivers and receivers, those who experience the effects of change. And that's true.

It may also be that we rarely list "humans" or "human creativity" because it's just universally assumed that humans both individually and collectively drive most change. It would be redundant to list "humans" in every driver.

But might it also be that we *forget* the immense power we wield as drivers of change? Perhaps we sense that the human contribution is being overshadowed by the "bigger" forces in the world. And there certainly are Goliath powers that drive change. But we forget that the human story is sprinkled with "David-like" stories. For those of you who may not be familiar with the biblical story. David is the young shepherd boy who killed a towering and experienced warrior named Goliath in a one on one face off.

Humans drive change. We have needs and wants. We make demands. We exploit opportunities. We create tools. We shape the environment. We build cities and fashion societies. We tell stories and play music. And, in the same way that ancient makers of fire touched us, what we do today touches the future.

Some call this unique human mechanism "creativity." The idea of creativity is gravid with the concepts of "choice" and "free will."

The idea of free will is controversial. There is disagreement about what free will is and even if it exists at all. But even proponents of a purely deterministic universe can't ignore this mysterious phenomenon. Some, like cosmologist Lawrence Krauss, have even conceded that, while he doesn't believe in free will, the world "behaves as if there is free will."

Human creativity suggests a thin fissure, a crack, in a purely cause-and-effect view of the world.

While "free will" implies certain philosophical beliefs, "choice" is eminently practical. "Choice" happens when humans express their free will in thought, word, or deed. It contrasts starkly with the sort of "choice" other animals exercise.

Living things "choose" between options that face them in the wild. Predators select which prey animal to attack. Foragers choose between equally tempting foraging vectors. Mate selection, a variable that rivals natural selection, decides the lineage of the next generation. While choosing is a natural ability, *human* choice transcends instinct alone in an unprecedented way.

Some might see the differences in "choice" between the human animal and all others as a matter of degree. But at what point can we say that our choices are so different in consequences that it no longer makes sense to speak of the distinction in terms of degree.

A New Trinity

Human creativity has proven to be one of the most powerful drivers of change on Earth. Our power to drive change comes from culture, the patterns of receiving knowledge, beliefs, values, and behaviors from prior generations and transmitting them to future generations.

Culture lays on top of nature like hair on head. It cannot be separated from or explained without the natural processes from which it emerges, but neither can it be comprehended by or reduced to these same forces. It is a layer of human design.

Culture can be seen at a rudimentary level in other animals, such as the way hunting techniques are learned and passed along by groups of Killer Whales (aka Orca). Certain pods of Orca demonstrate hunting techniques acquired from their ancestors that are not practiced by other pods. In other words, they are not purely instinctual techniques.

The Orca innovate, remember, and transmit knowledge through the generations.

A more recent find is the emerging "fashion" sense among chimpanzees. Started by a Zambian chimp named Julie in 2010, this behavior has seemingly caught on. They're putting grass in their ears.

So while culture may not be unique to us, for humans cultural evolution is exponentially rapid. In two million years we progressed from our breakthrough of making fire to sending humans to the moon on a column of smoke and a pillar of fire.

We evolved from our status as just one more creature dependent on its ecosystem to a place of stewarding and protecting all ecosystems. (This is reminiscent of the Genesis poem of creation in which humankind are guardians of the biosphere. Is this the prophetic power of poetry?)

The powers of natural selection may have brought humans so far, but the power of cultural creativity has brought us even farther faster. Human creativity forged a way past a life based on instinct alone.

We are developing a moral sensibility beyond the basic needs to survive and procreate. We create art and religion to express (and ideate) the meanings we read into the world we inhabit. We organize our social worlds according to what we value. And we are discovering that we can choose against the forces of natural selection. We can carve out a path of our own design, an option not available to any other creature that lives in this garden we call Earth.

Now we stand at a new threshold. Technology, which has been an extension of humanity since prehistory, has taken on a life of its own.

If our cultural evolution has left our genetic evolution in the dust, the exponentially rapid rate of technological evolution is leaving our cultural evolution behind. (And if we define "life" as anything that evolves, we may soon discover that our technology is alive).

Soon enough, our technology may begin its own evolutionary path as we design self replicating robots with the capacity to redesign and improve themselves. We will be sandwiched between two emergent systems: the biosphere and the Technium.

This trinity — our biosphere, our culture, and our technology — are inseparably intertwined. The rise of culture as a means of transmitting wisdom, creating values, and pursuing meaning, lies sandwiched between two incredibly generative forces.

In the same way that we learned to swim in the currents of the biosphere and are beginning to manage our purely instinctual nature and creatively work towards a more human world, we must now turn upon the rapid current of technological change and enter it with wisdom, values, and meaning or risk a future that is less than human.

Embedded within a life-creating orb called Earth, we are developing the technologies to be a life-creating force ourselves. Here on Earth, we must echo the creation symphony of Genesis chapter one and make life thrive. And as we unlock the secrets of life on Earth, we will hold in our hands the secrets to the future of life in the universe.

As we begin to export life, to colonize nearby planets like Mars and they become our stepping stones to the stars, the Anthropocene may extend itself throughout our solar system and beyond. Because we tattoo not only the Earth, but may make our mark across our solar system, we must decide what features will mark us.

Undertaking these challenges — to make the Earth thrive, to populate the stars, and to become human — will require communities of wisdom and courage. Not only are we the major drivers of change, are we also the major object of the change we need to drive?

Like the makers of fire of ancient times, we too stand between two worlds. Like them we will touch the future.

Chapter 5

Undercurrents

The Futures Program at the Hawaii Research Center for Future Studies was birthed within the school of political science. Part of their futures training includes imagining a colony on Mars and posits this question: Taking what we've learned from the human experiment on Earth, what form of government would we institute if we could begin with a clean slate on Mars?

It's a provocative thought experiment. What might be possible once we leave this blue orb called Earth? Could we leave our past hatreds and rivalries, claims to disputed lands, and other historical offenses behind us?

We might ask the same question for each of the STEEP domains (Society, Technology, Environment, Economics, Politics). What kind of economy would be ideal? What about religious and cultural mores? Would one worldview be preferred or might a plurality of perspectives be better?

But a disruptive question comes to mind. How do we create a new system of government or a new society and expect them to work better unless we create a new kind of human to populate them? Is it even possible to improve a human colony on Mars by tweaking societal, governmental, or economic systems without improving the humans themselves?

We are impacted by our environment. We are shaped by our culture. But we are not passive "reactors" only. We are also actors. We can shape an environment and a society by the strength of our character, our values and virtue, our ideas and morality... for good or ill.

How do we make new kinds of people for the new kind of future we seek? Soon we may attempt to design better humans at the genetic level. But will this lead to a Utopia populated by people who consistently choose good? Or, will it lead to a world without choice at all?

We'll need to ask questions like, If we could rid our species of a biological propensity for violence, should we do it? Might there be unwanted consequences? If we could eliminate human evil, should we?

A survey of human history reveals that the highlights of humanity hit during the darkest of times. The courageous Corrie ten Boom and her hiding place for Jews during the Nazi Holocaust, the compassionate Mother Teresa and her service to the lepers of India, the remarkable Nelson Mandela and his embrace of his enemies in South Africa are examples of people whose goodness shapes us.

If we were to eliminate violence and evil from history, and we lost the high points of our humanity, what kind of people would we be today? Who would we be without Moses, Abraham, Buddha, Teresa, Gandhi, and every person who bravely embodied what we mean when we say "human"?

What might we lose if we eliminate evil from the future? Would the evolution towards our humanity flat line? Would we miss out on future peaks that take our humanity to another level? Do we live in a world in which evil has a role even if it can't be justified?

*****

The leader in the field of human transformation is the ancient man, Jesus of Nazareth. Even today, twenty centuries after his life, hundreds of millions of people experience an inner transformation through exposure to him and his message.

The gospels tell us that once, when Jesus was teaching, a group of men brought a friend of theirs in hopes of a healing. Their friend was a paralytic. Upon seeing the concern of these men, Jesus says to the paralytic *"Son, your sins are forgiven."* (Luke 5.20)

This seems an odd thing to say. The presenting issue, the item of greatest concern, is that the man cannot walk.

There is an insight here about becoming human. Our greatest needs are not biologically enhanced bodies, uninterrupted connectivity, or lifespans of hundreds and thousands of years. Becoming human requires that we experience forgiveness and reconciliation.

Somewhere on our evolutionary journey, we developed a moral sense. We developed the ability to read each others' minds, to sense each others' feelings. We began to experience empathy.

All of these things seem like positive developments. But a consequence of this development is the ability to feel what others feel when *we* have wronged *them*. These powers came with a sense of responsibility. Feelings of guilt, shame, and multidimensional relational rifts are a reality of our experience.

As a result, becoming human requires that we do painful things. One very hard thing is to acknowledge that guilt and shame may be signals. For example, feeling guilt may mean that we need to take responsibility for our words and deeds, and a sign that we need forgiveness. Our feelings of bitterness and resentment may be signals that we need to offer forgiveness to others. Forgiving someone that has wronged you can be a difficult thing to do. Accepting forgiveness is even more difficult. Forgiving yourself when you've wronged someone you love may be the most painful thing of all.

Unless we're able to engineer perfect people, whatever system or society we create, whether it be for the future colonization of other planets or for the future healing of our shattered relationships here on Earth, will need to include a process of reconciliation.

Perhaps we will be able to bypass the need to reconcile by denying our "programming" to choose freely. But we may, without intending it, eliminate a miracle in the making: a human with choice who chooses to do right things.

If the story of Cain showed us a God powerless before the choice of one human, then Jesus amplifies that powerlessness. In Christ, God submits to the power of man. He does a painful thing: He forgives us. And then we crucify him.

That's the right order.

Christ isn't crucified in order that God may forgive us. He is crucified as a demonstration of his forgiveness.

Transformation did not begin at the pinnacle of power. It began at the bottom where the powerless are put down.

When it comes to change, it doesn't come from the top down. This is especially true about forgiveness. Forgiveness and its counterpart, repentance, cannot be demanded. They must be freely given.

Reconciliation isn't the concern of the empires of power. Governments are concerned with national self-interests and corporations are driven by profit. The empires of power don't want to enter a conversation about right and wrong, good and evil. They would prefer to avoid it by distracting us with entertainment, or pushing off judgment until the afterlife, or covering up the true impact of our consumption.

And we love being entertained. We love to dream about getting our later reward in heaven or when we win that lottery. We love the luxuries we enjoy and prefer not to know the ways it costs our biosphere, or the poor in the developing world.

But we hate it too.

Neither can this process rise from the bottom up. Too often the victim is focused on exacting revenge. This isn't how a process of reconciliation begins.

47

And often when the oppressed revolt and come to power, the end result is no better than what preceded it. The only thing that changes is who holds the power.

If atonement and reconciliation cannot come from the top down or from the bottom up, from where might it come? The process of reconciliation must come from the inside out.

That's why Jesus says, "Son, your sins are forgiven." He was saying that the healing of the planet had to begin on the inside. Forgiveness could only come from the inside of God. It can only come from inside of us.

Forgiveness cannot be imposed through external means. It has to begin as a creative act from within. And so it did, as an act within God.

Nothing else had to happen for forgiveness to be offered. God chose to forgive. Period. This is a painful act. And it continues to be painful until reconciliation finally becomes possible.

This touches on a profound force that is driving 21st century culture: Humans are longing for paths towards our humanity. And this path seeks reconciliation. This is a deep undercurrent at work at the micro level of our personal lives, the mezzo level of our societal lives, and the macro level of our global culture.

This longing explains why futurists ask questions about a hypothetical colony on Mars; why educated and motivated sales people go on vision quests; why high-powered corporate executives explore Zen Buddhism; and why intellectuals experiment with psilocybin.

This longing explains why, when the world's rarest parrot, the Spix's Macaw, went extinct in 2000 in its native Brazil, and only 76 were known to exist in the world, all in captivity, Sheik Saoud bin Mohammed bin Ali al-Thani began to purchase all known specimens of the species to rescue it from the edge of extinction.

It's why the country of Costa Rica wanted to do away with their zoos and let wild animals live wild, as "God intended."

It's why Millennials in the workforce volunteer so frequently for community improvement projects, and willingly work for less pay for an organization they believe in.

We are feeling our way forward through the wilds east of Eden towards a new path. And this new way has ancient contours. People want to feel connected. And not only to one another but to the Earth.

We want to be "brought together." That is the meaning of the word reconcile: to bring back together. And the legacy systems and structures that we have inherited no longer give us the freedom to move towards this goal. The paths that polarized governments, exploitative economies, and margin-obsessed corporations offer are dependent on their histories. Humans in the 21st Century are looking to be loosed from this path-dependence and break free to new ways of becoming human.

*****

The longing for a new way to be human may be why so many in the USA, when polled about their religious affiliations, check the box "None." We call them "the nones."

About one-third of adults under 30 years old classify themselves as having no religious affiliation. But, though the media tends to send this message as its first impression, it's inaccurate to think of this one-third as atheistic. According to recent Pew survey,

Two-thirds of them say they believe in God (68%). More than half say they often feel a deep connection with nature and the earth (58%), while more than a third classify themselves as "spiritual" but not "religious" (37%), and one-in-five (21%)

say they pray every day. In addition, most religiously unaffiliated Americans think that churches and other religious institutions benefit society by strengthening community bonds and aiding the poor.

This is a *description* of reality. What meaning might we *discern* here? I know so many people of vibrant faith who classify themselves as "nones" because they're detaching from traditional religious institutions in search of something more authentic. This is especially acute in the Christian faith because one isn't born a Christian.

In the West, many have forgotten how, and more importantly, why earlier generations came to believe. I suspect that the rise of those who identify themselves religiously as "nones" may reflect the rise of a deeper spirituality as much as it signals an abandonment of the institutions of faith.

In a recent conversation, a very thoughtful 25-year-old expressed this sentiment: "Even if all the claims of Christianity are true, I wouldn't want to be a Christian." Some have moved beyond their faith in Western Culture and its religion, Christianity. Because this person had at one time been a believer, I asked if there was something about faith that she missed. She informed me that she still believed that God hears her and that she'd at one time heard from God. That hadn't changed. What had changed is that she was no longer a Christian.

Where might this phenomena of the nones be leading us? Does it portend a seismic social disruption? In many ways becoming a Christian today may include a turn away from Christendom and the traditional churches that developed during that time. In fact, during this season of disruptive change, following Christ, for some, will mean *not* becoming a Christian.

To make an analogy with the life of Christ, Jesus was crucified by the Romans, then buried by friends. On the third day, he walked among his disciples again, raised from the dead. There were three days of "space" and "time" between the death of Christ and the resurrection of Christ.

Many today may be followers of Jesus who live in the time and space after the death of the Christian religion but prior to the resurrection of an expression that doesn't represent exclusion of the "other." Rather than rely on truth claims issued by an institution, they will try to remember how to trust again. Rather than institutional, the future of the Christ-following faith will begin as relational.

I suspect that the future of the church may be different than we expect. Let's put this radically: The Catholic church isn't the church of the future. Neither is the Orthodox church. The churches of the Reformation are not the church of the future. Neither are the evangelical churches, nor the emerging church.

None of these expressions are the church of the future nor the future of the church.

To play on a saying of Jesus, these may be some of the seeds but we have not seen the tree. Some will fear the death of the seed. But if the seed doesn't die, it remains just a single seed. But if it falls into the ground and dies, then it will reproduce itself many times over. (John 12.24)

The search for a new way of becoming human is the zeitgeist of our times, and many of us are going back to zero and starting again. This is a new journey of discovery, a new time to seek, and our whole culture is on it.

*****

People in the 21st century are looking for ways to ignite that ancient tribal fire that gathered us around one life sustaining force and defined us as "human." This is a deep, driving force. If we don't understand this, we cannot understand the world kindling around us.

Mythic, romanticized, and fanciful?

Sure.

But changing the world doesn't begin with a plan. It begins with a dream.

I see humanity's collective longing for reconciliation pursued more and more in three undercurrents that suggest the contours of this dream:

- from "outsider" to "insider"
- from "above" to "within"
- from "against" to "with"

If human history were a musical score, in the past, these may been atmospheric sound. What is new is the way in which these are on a crescendo in the human experience, changing from significant but minor background notes of the past to the dominant melodies of the present. In the past, these may have been background noise. Now they drive the symphony.

From Outsider to Insider

There has been a progression in human history from an insular and exclusive "tribalism" towards an open and inclusive tribe that shares the warmth of its fire with every stranger. In other words, our sense of who is an "insider" and who is an "outsider" is changing.

In ancient days, those who belonged to the tribe or clan were insiders.

This idea of who is an insider or outsider would extend at times to a federation of tribes or clans. This cultivated the tribal-self.

This understanding evolved with the rise of nations. Now inclusion was no longer limited to blood ties, but by citizenship. Our identities extended themselves beyond the tribe to include anyone who was our countryman. This developed the citizen-self. But the nation-state is too small of a container for the world view that is emerging.

Religion broadened the circle of inclusion. Though still subject to ethnic identity (Irish Catholic, Italian Catholic, Spanish Catholic), Catholicism was the first truly international organization. It had, and has, one pope and one vast band of "insiders" with representation in almost every nation. The Catholic church was global long before globalization became a thing. This nurtured the faithful-self.

Worldwide, many people have a self-identity that transcends national and ethnic lines in the name of religion. The greatest global Christian movement in the 20th century was Pentecostal. This is the fastest-growing religious movement in history. The 21st century will belong to the offspring of the Pentecostals around the world who share a kindred experience of the spirit of Jesus. For Catholics, Pentecostals, and other Christ-followers, there is a rising sense of connection and belonging that transcends denominational identity as well.

Today another layer of inclusion is weaving its way across the world. Ubiquitous web-based connections support this longing for a personal identity that transcends the individual - the solitary self, the tribe - the tribal self, the nation - the citizen self, and religion - the faithful self. A sense of self that includes "friends" from all around the world is emerging, a social self. The social network Facebook has a multinational population that rivals China and India.

Having a growing and diverse web of so-called "friends" on social networks isn't the solution to loneliness or the key to world peace, but it's a signifier. It signals the trajectory for the human story.

In the past, nation went to war against nation. That may continue, but from now on it will continue in a context in which "friend" is called to war against "friend." That will be an increasingly harder sell. And it may be a harbinger of change.

What lies beyond the social self? Personal identification with Christ leads to the cosmic self, a self identity that recognizes that God is in Christ reconciling the cosmos to Himself. It sees the Earth as its polis, its city, and all the peoples as kindred spirits on journey together.

From "Above" to "Within"

More and more, we see ourselves less as "above" the natural world and more as "within" the natural world. While   civilization may have allowed us to forget our close connection to nature, ideas from evolutionary biology, environmentalism, and paganism are helping us remember. More than half of young adults under thirty feel a connection to nature and the Earth (58%).

Rather than "control" over the environment (and   "leverage" over other nations, and "power" over other people), many sense that we belong to the environment (and to each other).

The citizens of Costa Rica, for example, are discussing the closure of their zoos. They want, in the words of one observer, "all of God's creatures to live free." And entertainment complexes like Sea World are becoming less tolerable as we become more and more aware of the feelings, perceptions, and intelligence of the creatures with which we share the world.

We are becoming aware that the natural world is the womb in which our species is developing. We cannot poison it without poisoning ourselves. There is a longing to return to the harmony of the creation poem of Genesis one. Loving the Earth is an act of self-interest for we are of the earth.

From "Against" to "With"

Humans are pursuing more collaborative environments. The competitive and "tough love" environments and processes we've been used to are giving way to more nurturing processes. Some moms in the USA would rather have their kids play in little league soccer games in which "everyone" wins and feelings are protected. Creating the competitive environment that would help the USA win the World Cup isn't a driving passion in this shift. Making sure that everyone feels valued is.

To say that our sense of identity has evolved from "Against" to "With" isn't to say that we don't value and long for a unique community. We still want to belong to a team, and a winning one at that. But we want to be "with" each other instead of "against" one another. We just haven't quite figured out how to get there.

Another aspect of this movement is the return of "neighboring." This is a culture-wide phenomena that seeks to reverse the alienation of city life. City planners are thinking more about ways to create community within their cities. Consumers are thinking more about buying local. Churches are shifting from regional and city wide strategies to strategies for "doing life" with their neighbors.

We don't want to be against each other because of race, culture, gender, orientation, nationality, political party, political party, or religion. We want to be with each other. We don't want to feel far away from each other. We want to sit together and tell our stories around the same fire.

Chapter 6

Artifacts

In Barcelona, Spain, there is a remarkable structure called *Basílica de la Sagrada Família.* This structure provides an analogy for how the past, the present, and the futures interact. Its architect, Antonio Gaudí, was known for his passion for religion and nature. *La Sagrada Familia* was to be his magnum opus.

The church is designed to have eighteen towers of ascending heights beginning with a tower for Mary, the mother of Jesus, twelve for the apostles, four for the evangelists, and the tallest tower for Jesus.

Gaudí began work on the structure in 1883. It has a completion date of 2026. When Gaudí was asked why it would take so long to build this enormous and complex church, he answered, "My client isn't in a hurry."

Gaudí died in 1926 when the work was less than 25% completed, but the work continued. Ten years or so later the Spanish Civil War interrupted the project; it commenced again in the 1950s. Because of my interest in *La Sagrada Familia*, when I learned that Japanese sculptor Etsuru Sotoo would be lecturing on the challenges of continuing Gaudi's work, I flew to New York City to listen.

During the question-and-answer session he was asked about the tension between his artistic freedom and the constraints involved in working on someone else's piece.

This question is relevant to all of us. None of us works from a blank canvas. We manage businesses started by others. Even if we start our own business we do so in a market and an economy shaped by others. We do research in fields defined and developed by others. We bring a child into a world created by others, and into a family with a history written by others. None of us starts at the absolute beginning. We start in the middle.

Our world as we receive it is an artifact created by those who came before us.

An artifact is something that is shaped and made by man. It can refer to a tool or shard of pottery found in an archaeological dig. This is the usual use of the term. But, it's also useful as a reference to concepts. For example, our legal, political, economic, and familial models are artifacts left to us from persons and events gone by.

Examples of artifacts from the domain of society would be polygyny, a marriage relationship of one husband and many wives, or the nuclear family which is made up of husband, wife, and children. A political and economic example is communism. The music we score, the film we produce, the poems we write, the art we create are all artifacts of our time.

The things we create today — from smart phones to drones, from emotionally sensitive robots to same-sex marriage — are artifacts we leave for later generations. The Ford Museum in Detroit has a billboard that says, "Three hundred years and 26 million artifacts." Anything we create and use in the present could end up as an artifact in the hands of a future archaeologist. Everything around us might become a future archaeological discovery, a future artifact.

An archaeologist working in the field who finds an ancient artifact asks, "What can this tell us about the humans who left them and the world they lived in?" The enduring artifacts of today will tell the future something about us and help them understand who we are, what we believe, and what we value.

And we can turn the question around: what can these artifacts — the things that make up our world, the things becoming real today — tell us about worlds to come? They can hint of trends and tides, directions in which we can expect the futures to go.

They can also tell us about potential futures, ones too new for trends to support. For example, in 2010 Craig Venter unveiled the first artificially created synthetic life form. What potential futures does this event suggest? In recent years, the institution of marriage has been redefined. What potential futures might this suggest about human sexuality and the structure of future families and society? Over the last two decades we have made a shift from thinking of computers as smart machines to experiencing them as sensitive machines, even as companions. Combined with the exponential progress in robotics and prosthetics during that time, what possible futures might these artifacts suggest?

But do we really have the creative freedom to take the world as it is in a new direction? Or are we destined to repeat the bad habits of the past?

*****

Sotoo's response to the question about creative freedom and contextual constraint beautifully addressed this question. He answered that he felt more freedom when working within Gaudi's work than he would have if he had started from scratch. To be unbounded, he suggested, creates fear not freedom. Freedom, he added, isn't the absence of constraints. Gaudi's preexisting work, he suggested, gave him a curious sense of freedom.

The key to understanding constraints as freedom came from changing his point of view. To look *at* Gaudi's work, to grasp all of it in detail, was a daunting task. So rather than looking *at* Gaudi's work, he instead chose to look *at the direction in which Gaudi was going*. In other words, he looked for the trajectories.

Like Etsuro Sotoo received an unfinished work, we receive an unfinished world. We don't start from scratch. We are constrained by what has gone before. And, our world is so complex that if we simply looked *at* it in all its complexity we might experience paralysis. The world is so complicated, so broken, so dynamic, so full of possibilities and dangers, so systemically interdependent, that the task of looking *at* it, of comprehending it all at once, would be impossible. But what if we were to look *through* the world to where it might be going, where it could go, and to where we wanted it to go?

This shift of perspective applies to how we look at other artifacts as well. Faith leaders might ask themselves, What if instead of looking *at* the Bible and *at* the Church, we looked *through* them for future possibilities?

Critics and skeptics look at the problems in the biblical text. Advocates point to the positives in the text. But what if we were to hold both in tension and look for future possibilities *through* the text? Rather than repeaters of past mistakes, might we then become creators of the human future?

Salvador Dali, the famous surrealist painter and *paisano* of Gaudí said about the unfinished *Sagrada Familia*: "It would be a betrayal to even think of finishing the *Sagrada Familia*... without genius. Let it remain there, like a huge rotting tooth."

Would it not constitute a betrayal of future generations to even think of adding new levels to human civilization… without foresight, intention, and love? Without the kind of creativity that makes the Earth and human community thrive?

As Etsuru Sotoo suggested, freedom isn't the absence of constraints. Freedom is the ability to choose within our bounds. The world "as it is" isn't the problem, it's the opportunity. Constraints are the womb of creativity. The freedom Sotoo describes is the embryo of human creativity, the art of the unexpected choice, the surprising mutation towards life and beauty that emerges out of the seemingly random chaos of creation.

Chapter 7

Scouting the Future

Even though we were in the middle of a thunderous whitewater rapid, the pounding roar was muted. The force of the running water had pushed our raft up against a rock in the center of the river. Despite our efforts the raft capsized and we were all tossed overboard. Three of us ended up in an air pocket underneath the upside down raft.

What struck me was the quiet. It was like being trapped under one huge noise-canceling headphone. The roar of the rapid was muted but you could still feel it out there. The water underneath the raft also seemed calmer. Without freezing cold water smashing into your face, breathing was easier.

Life under the raft had a seductive quality about it. It felt safe.

In the same way that the triangle of combustion serves as a useful analogy for how change happens, white water rafting can serve as a useful analogy for the experience of moving through time towards the futures.

I knew that we needed to get out from within the air pocket and back into the whitewater. But it was relatively quiet and still under there. And I was tired. I wanted to stay put.

Many of us prefer life under the raft. We know there's a thunderous rapid out there. The sounds of it — through the television news, email, or the radio — seep into our muted space. But we prefer to wake up in the morning and believe that all is quiet and still.

Even leaders prefer this. After all, who needs complications?

But life under the raft is a temporary condition. And it doesn't reflect the reality of what is happening outside our little space. I looked at the other two rafters in the air pocket with me. One of them was my 15-year-old son, Michael.

He smiled in the way he does and ducked out of the air pocket. He may have been only a few feet away from me on the outside of the raft, but our experiences of the world immediately around us were now radically different. He was back out experiencing the thunder of the whitewater. I was in the whitewater too, hurtling down the cold river just as he was. But life in the air pocket let me pretend, for a moment, that I wasn't.

Like everyone that has gone before us, we are adventurers riding a whitewater rapid of time. We may be in command of the raft, but we don't control the river. And change can happen quickly on whitewater, especially in the fast section of river we call the 21st century.

That's why smart rafters follow the proverb, "when in doubt, scout." The last thing a rafter or kayaker wants is to come around a river bend and face an unsurvivable drop. If you don't know what's coming, get out of the river and scout downstream from the safety of the shore.

And that's the problem: we cannot get out of the river of time and scout from the shore.

How then can we prepare for what's around the bend?

*****

About fifteen years ago I took my two eldest children to visit their great-grandparents in El Salvador. I wanted them to experience first-hand a part of our immigrant journey. Because my grandparents lived in the same house on the slopes of the Volcano of San Salvador for well over fifty years, my kids were able to sleep in the same bedroom I slept in many years before, in the same house where my mother lived before me.

The waters of time were almost gentle there. They seemed to move much more slowly.

Even though my grandparents experienced incredible changes in the course of their lives, the rate of change of their era seems slow to us. If one looks back in time through the generations, it seems that history slows to a crawl. Sure, rapid change disrupted the human experience during the transition points of history such as in times of war. But overall, for large chunks of the past, grandson and grandfather would live in worlds the other could fully understand.

Not anymore.

Futurity took the form of my two kids, sitting on the front porch of my childhood home explaining email to their great grandparents. It was hilarious. One family, four generations, same front porch, different universes. The one generation could not imagine the world in which the other lived.

A lot can happen in the interval between a man's great-grandfathers and his great-grandsons. Let's take an example from one of the greatest social movements of the last two thousand years, the rise of the Christian religion in the West.

Roland Allen, in his book The Spontaneous Expansion of the Church, describes how Christianity grew during a period of some 280 years from small clusters of believers in Asia Minor that were persecuted by the Romans to a force so powerful that Roman soldiers carried shields with the cross of Christ on them.

That's an amazingly short interval for such wide-spanning cultural change. And leading from the future is largely about understanding and leading change in the present.

At the height of the Roman Empire in the 1st and 2nd centuries, the emperors entertained Romans by throwing Christians to the lions. At the beginning of the 4th century, as the Roman Empire eroded around him, Emperor Constantine changed his mind about Christianity.

How does an empire's mindset change so dramatically?

You set it on fire.

The raw materials of the Roman Empire made for dry tinder. Rome had created an empire-wide system of travel and communication. The empire had a unified language, Greek, that facilitated conversation and commerce. The power of the empire created periods of relative peace and stability for the region. Perhaps more importantly, the empire had lost its momentum. Its global reach started to recede and barbarians began to push back against their borders. The crumbling empire became a shadow of its former glory. It lacked a mission in the world and thus lacked a meaning for its existence. The future looked bleak. What at one time seemed eternal was turning to dust. The stage was set was for the wide reaching spread of a new idea.

The fuel of compelling new ideas and values emerged from the margins, from an out-of-the-way place known as Judea. The message barely made sense to Jews much less to Romans, but the communities formed by this message embodied a new way of becoming human. These communities embraced the poor, the diseased, the widow and the orphan. Those who understood the message shared it everywhere they went.

These new ideas ignited by the heat of Jesus' leadership burned like spreading embers in the new communities of faith, setting the Roman Empire on fire. In the end Rome finally relented, accepting the new brand already seared into its hide: the Holy Roman Empire.

While the speed of change in the ancient Roman Empire seems incredibly fast, it doesn't compare with 21st century speeds of change. In the 20th century, the Soviet Union was a global superpower and the main political challenge to the

United States. The atheist empire was born in 1917, reached its zenith by mid-century, and by the late 1980s had disappeared into the mist of history. It emerged so quickly, few saw it coming. It collapsed so quickly, few saw it going.

This is one of the first things we must accept as we travel within our fast section of river. Change today happens at an unprecedented rate. The shape of the future is fast.

In fact, the accelerating speed of change - and our consciousness of it - is a core element of the 21st century human experience. Our section of the time-river is accelerating. This is a *description* of our reality.

We can expect that it will be even faster downstream. This speed means that we must simultaneously swim in the fast moving white water and scout downstream. Whatever happens now — whether a beautiful idea or a deadly virus — can spread globally at tremendous speed.

Think about the news cycle. Twenty years ago if you worked for a news magazine, the news cycle was weekly or even monthly. If you worked for a newspaper, the news cycle was daily. Every morning the newspaper hit the stands with the day's news. The best newspapers offered a Late Edition as well, on the newsstands in time for dinner. Today, the news cycle is minute by minute. Stories pour in from around the world as they happen and are sent out around the world in seconds via social media. News is available on demand, in real time.

And the changes we experience are not trivial. In the domain of society, the definition of family is changing, the definition of marriage is changing, the reality of privacy is fading, and even our sense of identity is rapidly evolving. Soon robots will be serving us in ways only humans once did. Big data will create personal marketing profiles so precise that it will not only know what we want, it will know what we are going to want before we do.

Some wonder, Is there anything we can do to slow things down?

Others ask, How can we speed this thing up?

Either way, it feels like we are picking up speed as we race towards tomorrow.

One thing you learn about rafting in whitewater: If you ever get thrown overboard in a rapid, the first thing you want to do is get on your back with your feet in front of you. That way, you'll hit any rocks feet-first, able to absorb the shock and push around them without injury, maintaining enough control to steer your course through the rapids.

In our time of rapid change, what's the equivalent of traveling feet-first?

Chapter 8

Weak Signals

Riding the rapids feet first means staying alert for possible obstacles that lurk immediately ahead in the river. Possible rocks in the river of time include those weak signals that happen beneath the awareness threshold. A weak signal is anything that happens that isn't widely noticed but which foreshadows a potentially high-impact and wide-ranging change. It's like a submerged rock in the river, hard to see until you are nearly upon it. If you fail to see it, it can catch you by surprise. The awareness threshold describes the point at which an event becomes more widely known.

Imagine if we could travel in time to Asia Minor around 50 AD. The Christian movement was only twenty years old. This is so early in the faith's history that it 's still a sect within Judaism. We visit a gathering of believers and witness their worship. We follow them as they go about their daily work during the week and listen in on their conversations.

Without the benefit of hindsight, would we correctly detect this social phenomena as a "signal" of up-and-coming transformative culture change?

I'm pretty sure that even the followers of Jesus living in 50 AD had no idea they were part of a movement that would change the Empire. They probably imagined that God would soon bring history to an end, spare them from extinction, and vindicate their faith in Messiah Jesus.

As time travelers to the first century, I think we too would easily have missed or even dismissed this small movement as being of no consequence for the future.

Except that we are from their future. We know what happens.

Nascent Christianity would have been an extremely weak "signal." Without the knowledge that change can come from unexpected places and unfold in unexpected ways, observing the newly-formed 1st-century Christian communities with no foreknowledge of their rise to prominence, we may have dismissed this movement as an up-and-coming force that would transform that ancient culture... and which continues to inform our own 21st century world.

In our culture of rapid change, riding the rapids feet-first means cultivating an eye for weak signals. Even if we never spot them we can know they're out there and just knowing this makes us more prepared.

In the practice of strategic foresight, this attention to weak signals is called "horizon scanning." It's the step beyond studying trends. A trend and the expected future it suggests can easily rigidify the imagination, becoming the only future a person is able to see. When the human imagination rigidifies, it becomes less able to respond to change when it comes. And disruptive change will come. The value of horizon scanning is that it's motivated by a readiness for change and inspired by an imagination filled with possibilities.

Because riding the rapids feet-first is all about being prepared for change in the present, there has never been a time when scouting downstream, looking for obstacles in the river of time, scanning for weak signals has been more necessary.

Change often comes from outside our normal field of vision, from the margins. In this environment, spending all of our time inside our silos is a dangerous activity. Step out and listen to what artists and radicals are saying for signs of social change. Scan the specialists journals for hints of new scientific thinking and technological breakthroughs. Look for that data that just doesn't fit. Keep track of what's happening in bellweather cities and countries. Pay attention to media for it's the 21st century tribal fire around which new stories are told and future culture is created.

Gandhi was not on anyone's radar when he moved from South Africa to India. John the Baptist and Jesus appeared seemingly out of nowhere and inspired a social change that still continues to blossom. Anti-Immune Deficiency Syndrome (AIDS) entered mainstream society from the margins of civilization.

Widen the radar of your attention.

Somewhere in the world, in a lab that is off the grid, something totally unexpected may have happened that will change the way the rest of us see the world. Watching for weak signals may not tell us which future will emerge, but it will keep us alert to the fact that the future that happens is often not the one we expect.

That alone is a super power.

Chapter 9

Mysterious Human Behaviors

Every now and then we hear reports of whales stranding themselves on shore. Why they do this is a mystery. There isn't anything on shore that might benefit them-- only death awaits them there. If beaching became a trend among any species of whale, it would have huge implications for their future.

There are so many *human* behaviors that might qualify as the equivalent of whales beaching themselves. Two equally mysterious "beaching" behaviors among humans carry huge implications for the futures they portend.

The first is the loss of a desire in the West to have children. While this is more commonly expressed in public among affluent urbanites, it's a demographic reality culture-wide.

Demographically speaking, the number of births per household needed to maintain a population is 2.1. The rate of births per household in the West has already dropped below this number, and birth rates are in a steep decline.

This trend is especially acute in Japan, where population decline is a crisis. (Japan isn't geographically part of the West, but it's well-developed and modern like the Western democracies and I believe it serves as a bellwether for the mysterious behaviors I'm discussing).

The second mysterious behavior is the loss (among a test group of young Japanese) of a desire to have sex. This isn't a trend but more of a "weak signal." In fact, this may be just an anomaly. That's why it's interesting.

The loss of desire to have sex as reported from Japan may not be a trend or an issue either in Japan or elsewhere, but it's a phenomena noteworthy enough to get some print, and it doesn't take much imagination to see its implications.

The desire to have children, and to have sex, with or without thought of children, are biologically embedded instincts. Would not the loss of these desires run counter to our natures? If these attitudes and behaviors became trends, what kind of future would they create?

*****

One of my favorite movies is *Children of Men*. The premise of the movie is that couples, for some unexplained reason, can no longer bear children. It's a dystopian vision of a future with no children, and thus, no hope.

An essay from the New York Times, Opting out of Parenthood with Finances in Mind, made me wonder if the reverse is also true. Is the loss of hope tied to loss of a desire to have children?

The essayist, a married, affluent, urbane young woman, writes about the economic sacrifices of having children. According to her, when she explained the article she was writing to other mothers, their words to her were: "good for you."

Not exactly the kind of mothers I'm used to.

This affluent person stands in stark contrast to those who in times of greater scarcity than our own would say, there's always food for one more. This affluent person isn't wrestling with the costs of feeding one more mouth. She's wrestling with the costs of affluence.

But what stands out from her essay isn't the economics of having children. What stands out is that she could find no good reason for having a child. Isn't this an ironically impoverished view of life? In fact, how is this a view of life at all and not a view of the *end* of life?

I'm sure the essayist is a fine person, but this article made me ask a dark, dark question about the worldview she suggests. I have to ask, What if children were free, a dime a dozen? Would she and her husband (who is preoccupied with the way humans tax the planet), find a reason or the space in their lives for a child?

I wonder, how similar is the worldview of this essay to that of Toni Vernelli, who aborted her child to save the planet, or that of Emily Letts, who filmed her abortion to show what a positive experience it can be?

I'm sure there's a world of difference between them all as individuals. But there seem to be larger cultural questions here. Is Western culture on a descent into an "end of life" worldview similar to the one described above? Is our culture concluding that having children just isn't worth the trouble?

If demography is destiny, then might it be the destiny of the West to disappear? Will we have our very own "Children of Men" moment?

This is a description of our reality, of what's happening out there. What meaning might be discerned here? Earlier generations delighted in the birth of a child. Some today will argue that the desire to have children is an evolved instinct. True. The desire to procreate, they may postulate, should be mitigated by the needs of the planet.

Is this the selfish justification that comes with affluence? Or, do the young somehow intuit that they live at the twilight of modern society and from this deep lack of hope feel nothing worth sharing and passing on to a new generation? Or, perhaps, like some animals and insects anticipate incoming natural disasters, might this younger generation of humans be better equipped to feel an oncoming extinction event and thus the desire to reproduce is neutered? Or has the loss of a religious view of life so disoriented us that we cannot be bothered with even the most basic evolutionary compulsions towards life? (The irony of that last question does not escape me.)

Is it a good thing now to *not* have children? At least, since some have seemed to have lost the natural instinct of it, it may indeed be a good thing... until we rediscover a reason to live, to enjoy living, and to love life enough that we want to be part of sharing the experience.

*****

Here's another even stranger symptom of the same malaise. Not only did Japan, with a fertility rate of 1.4 and lower, have fewer births in 2012 than any previous year, young people in Japan have stopped having sex. Just in case you read what your brain thought should appear in the text, let me put an emphasis on the key word: Stopped.

You can't even get to the question of should we or should we not have children, if you despise the physical contact that creates them.

Just when you thought impossible things never happened, the impossible appears:

"A survey earlier this year by the Japan Family Planning Association (JFPA) found that 45% of women aged 16-24 'were not interested in or despised sexual contact.' More than a quarter of men felt the same way."

This survey contradicts what we understand about humans. That's what makes it interesting. So, it feels weird to ask this but, could *not* having sex become an epidemic in Japan? Could it become a global epidemic? Remember, what we're practicing here is an alertness to weak signals. This is a solitary signal that has not risen to the level of a "trend" or an "issue" but it offers us the opportunity to imagine alternative futures.

In reaction to this news from The Guardian (also reported by The Observer), *The Week* published an article titled "Everything You Need to Know about Japan's Population Crisis." In it, they argued:

"The British newspaper The Observer recently caused an international stir by reporting that Japanese youth have lost interest in sex. The sensationalist conclusion was mostly based on a single statistic: a survey that found that 45 percent of women and 25 percent of men ages 16 to 24 said they were not looking to have sex. The article also cited the phrase sekkusu shinai shokogun, or "celibacy syndrome," as if it were a major trend. In reality, more Japanese singles are having sex than in past decades. In 1990, 65 percent of unmarried women and 45 percent of unmarried men had never had sex; today, the figures are 50 percent and 40 percent, respectively. 'Of course Japanese have sex,' Asian studies professor Jeff Kingston told Bloomberg.com. 'If the number of love hotels is any barometer, it seems like many are getting plenty of it.'"

The Week makes clear that the JFPA's study is the very definition of a "weak signal." In other words, the 45% of women and 25% of men who said they were not looking to have sex isn't yet a trend or an issue. Again, just to be clear, a weak signal may never rise to the level of being an issue or a trend. This survey may simply be an anomaly.

But while the "celibacy syndrome" has not reached "syndrome" status, might it be a signal of something that is lurking just below the surface? What if this gained momentum and became a social issue? What would this portend for Japan's near future? What if this type of attitude rose to the level of a trend and became a social issue across the West? What future scenarios might we imagine?

Following this train of thinking will not help us predict the future because, again, the future cannot be predicted. It does, however, exercise our powers of imagination and cultivate mental fluidity. This enhances our capacity to deal with complexity.

For an organization or business whose strategic plan lays vulnerable before a rapidly changing landscape, it creates a state of mental preparedness and opens the door to options. These are superpowers that come into play when change does happen, regardless of the change.

In their article, *The Week* focused on a fact of nature: the young want to have sex. That's not news. *The Observer*, in their article, unearthed an interesting weak signal: an unusually high number of women and men expressed a disinterest in experiencing sex. That's worth noting.

One can see that *The Week* entirely misses the point and quite likely misdiagnoses the data. Like every culture that is emerging from more traditional mores of abstaining from sex until married, poll numbers may indicate that people more freely admit to having sex today than yesteryear. That may reflect changing behaviors, but it might also reflect changing cultural mores. More relaxed cultural mores towards sexual behavior makes the results of the survey not less but more startling. *The Week's* comments don't even begin to explain the unexpected picture captured in *The Observer's* one statistic.

What's going on here? (Assuming the survey was not flawed, which, of course, it could have been...) What meaning might be *discerned* underneath this *description* of reality?

Could this discovery signal something positive? Are we finally gaining mastery over our naturally-evolved instincts? Could this anomaly signal nothing but a narrowly contextualized and temporary mood of these young people? Or, might this phenomenon signal a surrender to meaninglessness? Are these attitudes symptoms of the dis-ease of hopelessness that can attack all humans anywhere at anytime? Might this (coupled with new technologies) pave the way towards a future of childbearing unrelated to sex?

Japan is a global leader in the commercial sex industry, featuring nightclubs with "female robots" that "wink and wave," a tech-savvy population whose young men are addicted to online porn and who "date" online avatars. This weak signal is embedded in a society that has set a high bar for the objectification of women and the dehumanization of sexual intimacy.

Does this combination of misogyny and technology offer a glimpse of a possible future for the world?

This century we will see in the USA dramatic acceptance of the legal sex industry. The porn industry will come out of the closet and enter the mainstream. Virtual reality may drive more young men into fantasy worlds. What future might we anticipate if this one survey, this one weak signal, proved to be more than just an anomaly?

At the very least, we can say that not having children and not having sex are biologically dead ends. Japan is already in a crisis. Unless something changes, the Japanese may move beyond being an "endangered culture" to an extinct one.

Are humans who stop having children, who start killing their children, or who start hating sex, the equivalent of diseased whales beaching themselves on the shore? Or, are they enlightened?

Has something about living, about life, stopped working in them? Or, are they more ecologically responsible?

Whatever the case, these behaviors run counter to the most primal drives within us.

In the negative, we can postulate that human societies start by dismissing Spirit or Meaning. Without God to blame this may lead to hating life itself. In the positive we can experiment by breathing faith, hope, and love into a culture that can't seem to figure out why humans are worth saving, worth bringing into the world, or even worth touching.

Chapter 10

Kinds of Futures

Human creativity can be restorative, healing the world. It can also be generative, opening new possibilities for the world. Leading from the future means stoking the human desire to heal until it burns more fiercely than the human drive to destroy.

So, what if, instead of only looking *at* the world, we took a cue from Sotoo's perspective on the *Sagrada Familia*, and looked instead *at the directions in which the world could go*? How could we begin?

Leaders could begin by asking three questions.

The first question is, What are the **possible** futures?

This question opens the mind. This is where we are set free from the mindset that "whatever will be will be," that "things never change," and "there isn't anything new under the sun." It's an act of inhaling possibilities.

Science fiction is a tool for imagining such possibilities. It's remarkable how much science fiction has anticipated **the events** and breakthroughs that created the future: robots, genetic engineering, space travel, cyberspace.

Arthur C Clarke said, "Any sufficiently advanced technology is indistinguishable from magic." Our routine and ordinary lives would appear supernatural to humans who lived just a century ago. And we are just arriving at the very beginning of our technological powers.

Imagining possible futures is also where we must face both our deepest fears and our greatest hopes. This exercise shakes us loose from the default mentality of believing in "the" future. This is where the "black swans," the unexpected futures that are unlikely to happen but would change everything if they did, are placed on the table of possible tomorrows.

A second question narrows the field. What are the **probable** futures?

This question focuses the mind. This is where we begin to "scan the horizon" for signs of change. We listen to pop culture (movies, music, social media, etc) to hear what it is saying. We focus our reading and research, we become more alert to that unusual article, we step outside of our industry and look for developments across the TESA (Technology, Entrepreneurship, Society, Arts) or STEEP (Society, Technology, Economics, Environmental, Political) domains. In other words, we collect Fuel for making fire.

This is where we construct narratives that make clear how certain futures could emerge from the Artifacts we are creating in the present. These narratives are a tool for imagining probable futures and are called **scenarios**.

If possible futures lay at the periphery of our imaginations, probable futures are a step closer towards the center. A scenario is a narrative that maps the pathways from where we are right now to where we could be in the future. This second question allows us to explore ways our deepest values might shape our decisions in a plurality of future tomorrows.

Within the sphere of the probable futures there are what we call the **expected** futures. Expected futures are the results of extrapolating trends. A **trend** is a continuous change in a variable over time.

For example, a much-noted trend today is the declining birthrates of the Western democracies. There must be 2.1 births per couple in order to replace a nation's population. If the number of births drops below this, a population will begin to decline. And that is a current trend in the west.

A trend suggests an "expected" future that will happen if nothing changes. And therein lies the danger.

Because trends can be extrapolated over long periods, their projections can be mistaken for future facts. But, as Peter Bishop, professor in the Strategic Foresight program at the University of Houston, reminds us, "there's no such thing as a future fact." We must never confuse the "probable" futures or even the "expected" future with "the" future.

Trends may lull us into a false feeling of certainty. The farther into the future one dares to extrapolate a trend, the less likely it becomes that this "expected" future will happen. This is because for trends to continue there must be no unexpected disruptions, no change in all the other variables that support the trend. But all those other variables are likely to change eventually, and many may change soon, and change quickly. We must beware the false security (or unwarranted despair) created by the "expected" future.

The third question is crucial: What is our **preferred** future?

This questions summons human energy. This is the leadership question. In the language of leadership this is called **"vision."**

A person with vision engages the imagination and develops a comprehensive sense of where we are and where we need to go. One tool leaders use to activate their vision is vision casting. **Vision casting** is the art of describing a compelling image of the future that invites others into the creative process. In this way, the leader, the seer of unseen things, creates a community of vision around this image of a mutually preferred future, and concurrently develops the new leaders this preferred future will require. Together, if successful, this community of vision will make the invisible visible.

With this question we are not willing to simply wait and "let the future happen." We become active and intentional because we recognize that our choices may influence which of the possible futures may emerge. Here we become creators. We recognize that we wield in our hands the power to create the future. This is the domain for makers of fire.

Some people "think" these three questions naturally, perhaps without even knowing it, because it's the way their minds are patterned. The rest of us must learn to ask these questions. All of us can grow in the ability to think in these ways. And all of us can develop skills to keep us abreast of the changes that are happening all around us.

Just to be clear, asking these questions doesn't mean you'll know the future. The future can't be predicted. It does mean that you'll be more ready for change in the present.

Chapter 11

Smoke on the Horizon

Demographics is one of the most reliable ways to imagine the "expected" future. One aspect of demographics is populations studies. We can project future population growth or decline by looking for trends within the birthrates. Are birth rates rising or declining, and at what rate? Are births distributed equally around the world? If not, where will most future humans come from?

In terms of population, it took the human species 250,000 years to reach the first billion. It took us just 12 years to add the most recent billion. In the next three decades we'll add nearly another two billion as global human population growth slows down. If you're 50 or older the world population doubled in your life time.

By the middle of the 21st Century, the world's population will reach the nine billion mark, unless something unexpectedly disrupts the trend.

In terms of religion, world Christianity continues to expand but the center has shifted from the west to Africa, Latin America, and Asia, where population growth is more robust.

As these nations rise, so will their versions of Christianity. Missionaries from the developing world are already present in the United States, where the European churches are in decline.

In terms of urbanization, migration patterns suggest that the Earth is becoming a city. And in terms of aging, patterns suggest that the world's population is getting older.

These are the smoke on the horizon. The smoke suggests a change in the demographic realities of the future.

In bullet points, the expected global future is

African — Half the world's births between now and 2050 will be African.

Spiritual — the world religions continue to grow, with Pentecostal Christianity centered in the nonwestern world leading the way

Urban — by 2050, 70% of the world's population will live in cities

Grey — by 2050, the average age of all humans will be 9 years older than it is now.

These represent trends which can be extrapolated into images of the "expected" future. But, again, the expected future must not be confused with "the" future. The "expected" future can be the future that is least likely to happen. Because in order for the expected future to happen the trends must continue without change. That requires a lot of faith in our age that is characterized by rapid change.

We may travel in time towards a trend, like following the smoke on the horizon in search of fire, only to experience a disruption and discover that the smoke on the horizon wasn't smoke at all. It was a moving herd kicking up dust.

What kinds of things could happen that would shatter our images of the expected future?

*****

As defined by Nassim Taleb, Black Swans are unforeseen events that have a disproportionately huge impact, and that seem predictable, even obvious, *after* they occur.

Examples of recent Black Swans would be the terrorist attacks on New York and Washington DC in September of 2001, the rise of Nelson Mandela, and the financial crisis of 2008. The attacks of 9/11 and the crisis of 2008 were after the fact considered by some to be predictable.

They say prediction is difficult especially when it comes to the future.

But according to Taleb, Black Swans are often accompanied by Retrospective Distortions, by a sense that we actually understand the event and ought to have seen it coming.

Change doesn't come to one area of life in isolation. This is because we exist in an interconnected system. So, when thinking about the future, it isn't enough to ask, "What happens next?" We must ask, "What happens because of what happens next?"

Over the course of the next century, we may see for the first time in history:

Resurrection — the "Jurassic Park" style return of extinct species

Extraterrestrial life — given the increasing number of Earth-like planets being discovered it's increasingly possible that we will discover life forms that we can recognize

Robust Human Rejuvenation — life spans that reach hundreds of years

The Colonization of Mars — starting in the mid 2020s

If thinking about the future means, in part, asking, what happens next?, then thinking systemically about the future means asking, what happens because of what happens next?

If demographics are a reliable way to envision an expected future, Black Swans remind us that expected futures are also unreliable. What kinds of black swans may be swirling around these futures that many have come to expect?

Some of these black swans may come from nature or from space. But some Black Swan may be the unexpected consequences of our actions. Human beings are creative and capable of bringing novelty and surprise to the human story in the form of new ideas, discoveries, and choices.

Beyond the smoke on the horizon suggested by the trends we mention in this section, let's also take a cue from Etsuru Sotoo and his work on Sagrada Familia and ask the question, where might the world be going?

Chapter 12

Trajectories

The Rise in the Status of Women

In Korea, if a woman gave birth to a daughter she would sometimes apologize. The depreciation of females isn't a thing of the past. Female infanticide is an ancient practice that was still practiced as recently as the 20th century in China due to its One Child policy.

But that is changing. Today, Korea, one of the new centers of global Christianity, leads Asia with a new attitude towards women and baby girls.

Here's the new trajectory: girls are of equal value to boys and deserve equal dignity, treatment, and opportunity to pursue personal happiness, community leadership, and social status.

This seems "matter of course" to many of you, but if you think it's the matter of course around the world and throughout history, you may want to rediscover the world we live in. Girls are still profoundly undervalued. This idea is a revolutionary shift in paradigms that's changing the world we live in right now. It's a description of a new reality.

But there are counter forces at work in the world. The rise and spread of cyberporn is shaping a generation of boys with unrealistic and animalistic views of sexual intimacy. The dehumanization of women advanced through this medium awakens the darkest desires of the human psyche. The world is still littered with clubs that dehumanize women. Soon the women in this dark world will be pushed even further down the ladder by gynoids — the female counterpart to androids — whose exaggerated bodies will appeal to men whose appetites have already been distorted by their online sex lives.

Emerging technologies from the world of gaming such as the Occulus Rift, which provides an immersive 360 degrees experience, will provide these dark forces even more virtual power.

What lies at the bottom of this rabbit hole? To put these dangers in stark terms, how will these dark forces ever be defeated when there will always be those who make their living by exploiting the vices and vulnerabilities of others?

The Rise of Human Dignity as Natural Right

The eradication of legalized slavery in the West in the last two hundred years, and the election of a Black American president, both point to a trajectory that is changing the world.

Here it is: all people deserve dignity, respect, and love.

The conversation on race in America, about which so many have clamored, has been taking place over the last couple of centuries and the good guys are winning. This battle, however, is far from over. Slavery is a growing global reality. Depreciation of others based on color, culture, and caste still happens, even in those countries that have outlawed slavery. This is a tectonic shift in paradigms that the whole world will need (and want) to get used to.

But there is more slavery today than ever before. It may be illegal in the west and beyond but slavery is far from eliminated. Even though Western culture no longer legally builds on a slave economy, the slave economy still thrives in the world upon which Western culture is built. The West is a light on a hill for women and children, free or slave, around the world. But, the slave trafficking industry is present in every corner of our world, even in our small towns. Again, to put this in stark terms: how will we ever defeat this dark impulse when our species has always practiced slavery when the economic conditions favor it?

The Fall of Human Dignity as a Natural Right

Yes, the exact opposite of trajectory number 2. While depriving dignity to any kind of person is no longer imaginable in some of the world today, there is a new world rising.

The race for genetic enhancements will be to the 21st Century what the race to space was to the 20th. Who will benefit from the emerging technologies that will genetically and electronically enhance humans? Who will be left behind? Will those with the economic means separate themselves from the rest of us over time by means of genetic enhancements? Will we create a new underclass of "organic" humans who are a different species from the new and more impressive kind of "enhanced" human?

Here's the trajectory: The weakest and most vulnerable among us should share (if they wish) in the benefits of the emerging new species of human we will create. And, as the species bifurcates into two distinct families of homo sapiens, those who do choose to be left behind should be protected against the future form of discrimination: species-ism.

The reverse application of species-ism, in which nonhuman animals are valued as much as humans, is also a factor. As animals gain more human rights and we begin to view the killing of animals not as killing but as murder, will we always choose to save the human animal when faced with a choice? This is not far fetched. Already there are many in the environmental movement who value the Earth or the natural world more than humanity.

We are making gains but we must remain vigilant. It may not take much to experience a global reversal in the status of women and in the expectation of human dignity as a natural right.

The Role of America by the 22nd Century

A final world changing trajectory to consider is the role of America in the world. There is a new term floating around China today that Americans should be aware of. The term is "leaving the dollar behind." One hundred years ago the British Pound was the world's reserve currency. Today it's the American Dollar. But the global economy is reeling and the Chinese in particular are floating the idea of creating a "backup" currency to the dollar. What will be the global reserve currency by century's end?

The image of the USA as the sole global superpower, as the top of the heap, may be eroding. This idea resonates with those who believe that the American prominence has ended. Popular books, such as The Post-American World by Fareed Zakaria, point to a world that is moving beyond America in economic and cultural terms towards an eclectic global cultural mashup. We have experienced the expanding global reach of the Chinese economy and the growing global presence of Indian culture. There are blue jeans in the farthest reaches of the Earth, Chinese restaurants in every small American town, and hipsters in India.

Others, like George Friedman (The Next 100 Years), assert that the 21st century will be the American century, at least in geopolitical terms. And, even though current developments in Africa suggest that it's being recolonized by the Chinese, the United States alone, like the British of the 19th and early 20th century, will rule the seas into the foreseeable future.

In order to maintain its global dominance, the United States will not need to win any wars. All that will be needed is to prevent the rise of another hegemony that can challenge its place as the supreme power over the Earth.

In broad strokes, when it comes to consumerism, movements towards democracy, and models of opportunity for the least powerful in society, it seems that the world is coalescing around American values. If this is true, then the future of Western culture may be the future of the world.

If so, how will we shape our culture and world in ways that reduces the dehumanization of women (and children), eliminates the economic incentives for treating humans as property, and elevates even the most marginal and vulnerable of people to the place of most cherished human?

The Earth is our *Sagrada Familia*. It's the unfinished world we have received. Perhaps we should leave it as it is, "like a huge rotting tooth." Or perhaps we can learn to celebrate when genius arises within our communities. The world was once dark and our ancestors, using nothing more than the materials found in the natural world around them and the imaginative genius that was within them, domesticated the power of fire. They changed the world for themselves and all of us who live in their future, a future they could not even imagine.

Chapter 13

Describing the Present

My grandfather was born in 1911. To put this date in perspective, the Wright Brothers had their first successful flight in 1903. In 1969, when my grandfather was fifty eight years old, Neil Armstrong walked on the moon.

The progress from the first airplanes to the manned lunar missions was gargantuan during his lifetime. Especially when you consider that his date of birth was closer to the assassination of Abraham Lincoln (1865) than it was to the Apollo mission.

Ask yourself this question: how much technological change will there be in your century (the 21st century) compared to my grandfather's century (the 20th century)? Will there be thirty, fifty, or eighty times more change?

According to the Pew Research Group, there will be a thousand times more technological change in the 21st century than we experienced in the 20th.

The domain of technology isn't the only source of disruption. After September 11, all of us know just how quickly human choice can change the world. Human creativity can bring light and warmth into the world. It can also make the world dark again.

It's a thunderous whitewater rapid out there.

Compared to my grandfather's century, the next century will be a blur. The worlds of science fiction and contemporary reality will continue to interweave. It makes me wonder. At today's accelerating rate of change, what will be the marvels (or horrors) that our grandchildren will be unable to explain to us?

But before we begin to imagine the possible wonders and horrors of tomorrow, the first ingredient in the Triad of Leadership is to describe and define reality today. So, beyond contemplating the game-changing trajectories of elevating the status of women world wide, establishing the value of each and every human being on the planet, and exploiting the status of the USA for the good of the world, let's scan this first section for one-word descriptors of the present and add some others to get a good feel for the Fuel around us. The present is a time of ...

SPEED

It's not just about change. It's about an exponentially rapid rate of change that is outpacing our wisdom to manage it.

UNCERTAINTY

Disease... The recent Ebola epidemic in Africa keeps before us the possibility of a real global pandemic lurking out there in our future.

Economic... Will the global economy ever stabilize?

Terror... when will that biological weapon activate?

Technology... Will AI make humans obsolete?

Environment... When will we experience that epic superstorm?

Extinction... a deadly combination of multiple factors such as stronger diseases due to our wide spread use of antibiotics combined with immense urbanizations that provide a moist organic incubator for a deadly and incurable virus coupled with airport travel hubs through which a virus can reach the world.

SOCIAL

By "social" we don't mean more relational but more media driven. Social media is the tribal fire around which the stories that shape our culture are being told.

ROBOTICS

Everything from drones taking to our commercial airways, to Pepper and Jibo, the world's first affectionate and family robots.

DISINTEGRATION

Traditional social arrangements are dissolving. For the first time since the collection of the relevant census data, Singles make up more than half of the adult population in the USA. Progressives have a vested interest in keeping Americans single because single women tend to vote progressive and married women tend to vote conservative. In Los Angeles you'll hear the term "Starter Marriage" to describe first marriages, the expectation being that the first marriage will dissolve and that they will upgrade to more permanent arrangements in second and third marriages later.

"NEIGHBORING"

We may not be able to do anything about the way the world and its traditional institutions are falling apart, but we can make a difference in our neighborhood. That's why there is a stream of people who are "going local." Many people want to shop in locally-owned businesses, buy locally grown food, have a neighborhood church in a local home, and know their neighbors. It's a way of simplifying life in an increasingly complex world.

DISPARITY

There is a growing concern to close the gap between the poorest one billion and the rest of the world. Social Entrepreneurship and "triple bottom lines" are the new discussions about the future of business.

ECO-COMPASSION

A step beyond eco-consciousness, eco-compassion expresses human compassion for the natural world which features the elevation of other animals to the status of "neighbor" and sometimes includes the devaluation of humans.

SEARCH

As exemplified by the drive to colonize Mars, our pursuit of a new way to become human, and the well liked google search field.

SELF-HATRED

Some people are more concerned with nature, and how people tax the planet, than they are about people themselves. Others think of children as a commodity one might or might not want. This is a huge reversal of values, a hatred of one's own species.

WONDER

As we discover more and more about our universe and ourselves, and as we push the limits of what we, as a species, are able to accomplish, we will at the same time marvel at how little we know and the "why," the meaning of conscious existence.

SLAVERY

Beyond the mainstream acceptance of a dehumanized sexuality and the global growth of the legal sex industry, slavery is still a part of the global economy.

VIOLENCE

Drug cartels in South America, political corruption in Mexico, Islamic suicide bombers, the ambition to extinguish Israel, the desire for an Islamic hegemony to challenge the West, the longing for freedom in Hong Kong as China clamps down, the aspirations of a Russian empire, the possible remilitarization of Japan, the proliferation of biological weapons of mass destruction, racial conflicts at the national and neighborhood level, the list goes on. Will a non-killing society ever be possible? (Perhaps the disciples of Jesus who flow in the nonviolent stream of the Christian religion may be the only existing society with the resources to accomplish this).

ERASURE

Our age is a time of tension between forces that desire to "undefine," redefine, and define. For example, some today object to announcing the gender of a new born— "It's a girl!"— because they feel this limits the possibilities for the child. Don't be surprised if, in the future, someone challenges the information that goes on a birth certificate. They may argue that including gender violates an infant's rights to a future of their choosing. The "Undefiners" want to leave things nameless, to erase definition, to "undefine." As another example, in the past, relationship experts wrote books and gave speeches to help couples understand the differences between men and women. Today some are finding it necessary to argue first that there is such a thing as men and women.

But there are also signs that rather than undefine, some want to redefine. For example, some want to redefine marriage. And family. And self identity. Naming creates categories. Naming is an important task. It tells everyone else what it is they're supposed to see. It establishes an order. Some want to redefine the world so that it conforms to their vision of it.

But we are not unanimous on what those names should be. Others want to reinforce standing definitions. Boys are boys and girls are girls. There is such a thing as a man and a women. These aren't choices. Marriage is what it has always been. They may be open to new names for new phenomenon, but they don't want to rename what already has a name.

The first task of a leader is to describe and define reality and it's never been more challenging than it is today. It's a century of tension.

This is the fuel that is settling around our feet.

*****

When I set out on my first whitewater rafting adventure on California's infamous Kern River, I sat for the safety talk that is required before you enter the waters.

I'll never forget our guide's first words: "Whitewater rafting is inherently dangerous."

You could feel the emotional spike among us newbies.

After a dramatic pause she continued, "And that's why you're here."

My friends and I smiled and nodded our heads. It was like she'd read our minds.

A few years later, when my son Michael turned fifteen, we enrolled in a white-water guide school. As an added value, the week-long experience included three days of swift water rescue training. That's how I ended up in the air-pocket under a raft.

We learned that week that there are a lot of ways to die in a river. Our first guide, who had given us that safety talk those years before, had not been kidding. Rafting is inherently dangerous.

It was in Guide School that we learned the proverbial wisdom of white water guides: when you're rafting a section of river you don't know, get out and scout. You don't want to come around a bend in the river and lead a crew over a waterfall.

In terms of history, we can know the section of river we have already rafted. We know the past. In terms of futurity, the future is a section of river with which we are not familiar. And when in doubt scout.

There lies the gravest danger of this river of time we all travel. We cannot get out of the flow. There is no escaping the current, the constant movement forward. There is no shore from which to scout what lies downstream. That's why riding the rapids of time requires absolute attention to the present moment, to what is happening right now.

What signals is the river giving us that foreshadow what may lie ahead? What weak signals are we receiving? These are not signals from the future. They are signals from right now that have implications for the future.

Humans have always wanted to know the future. We have sought out fortune tellers, listened to prophets, looked for secret formulas in search of such knowledge. But it's our human condition to travel the river of time without knowing what lies around the bend.

As your guide to the future I am obligated to tell you: thinking about the future can be scary because this river we're on is inherently dangerous. And, I suspect, that's why you're here.

Change was coming to the clan and she knew it. But how could she show it? It had taken her two fire seasons to see it herself. The smoldering coals could live within the empty skull but, like everything else that lives, it needs to feed. And if fire could be kept alive, perhaps it could even live among them.

She quickly collected embers and placed them within the skull. She placed a thick fur on her left hand and, with the reverence due to deity, she lifted the skull with her hand using her sharpened stick to support most of the weight.

As she walked with the skull towards the hunting party, the flow of air entered through a hole in the skull and the embers ignited into flames. She stopped startled and the flames slowly dwindled. She began to move, the flames flared up, and again she stopped. Slowly she made progress until she caught up with the hunting party.

They peered into the skull and listened as she explained her vision. She fed the fire some dry grass. It was hard to explain because they did not yet have sounds for such a thing.

It is like all living things, she thought. *It eats and breathes.* "If we care for it," she said to them, "perhaps it will make a home for itself among the clan." All the way home they cherished the skull, took turns carrying it, and feeding it. Finally, they could see their shelters on the horizon. By the time they arrived, the fire in the skull had died. As the day ended and the darkness of night approached, she squatted again, reflecting on the events of the day.

As they told the story to the clan, not everyone understood. But, they trembled at the thought that the gods were coming and would soon make their home among them.

When the universe makes you wonder, all is as it should be.

- Varekai (Cirque du Soleil)

OXYGEN

Chapter 14

Drowning

Just for the joy of it, I jumped out of the raft and into the white water. Even though I was in training to be a guide, I was still relatively new to the sport. Unknown to me, that stretch of the run had a beautifully spaced train of waves.

There's a technique for breathing in these conditions. As you might imagine, taking a breath as one rises on a wave seems natural. Makes sense. But sometimes instinct can mislead you. What actually happens is that, while you do rise with the wave, your head doesn't always fully break the surface.

In my case the tip of the wave slapped me in the mouth just as I took in air and I swallowed tons of water. As I broke through the wave, the water dropped quickly and brought my upper torso out of the water. So, when I should have been breathing, I was coughing and getting rid of the water.

My need for air, now compounded, grew. But I took hope because I was rising on the next wave. I knew I couldn't afford for that to happen again. I waited until I hit the top of the wave and inhaled another mouthful of water. I broke through the wave, coughing out water with my last remaining breath.

I'd missed two breaths now. My need for air was desperate. This was no time to panic. Fortunately, I was rising on the next wave. This was it, I had to keep my composure and give this my best effort. So, as I approached the crest of the wave I harnessed all my remaining energy and extended myself as far as I could in pursuit of that desperately needed breath.

Have you ever been deprived air? I can tell you that a lack of air rises quickly to the top of things that need immediate attention.

In our triangle of combustion, Fuel represents the "What?" and Oxygen represents the "Why?" Oxygen is the second ingredient needed to create a burning event. Meaning is the second ingredient needed to understand social change. And discerning meaning is a key to 21st century leadership.

The human search for meaning is like our need for air.

Whether prompted by the emergence of Artificial Intelligence, the discovery of extra terrestrial life, or the growing understanding of the emotions experienced by other animals, the central question of the 21st century will be, What does it mean to be human?

This isn't a question of where humans fit on the evolutionary chart. It's not about "what" we are, but about "why" we are. It's a question of meaning.

Meaning and Purpose

One way to know what something means is to understand its purpose. In order to understand the meaning of a sound, for example, we need to know why it's used.

Let's say you're visiting the midwestern United States in April and you hear a loud wailing sound. A native to the area will know the meaning of the siren. They'll know it's April, the heart of tornado season. They'll understand that this sound is part of the local severe weather safety program. It's a tornado warning. And they'll know what to do. They'll hurry indoors or underground if possible because they know that a leviathan has broken through the skies.

But if you're from another part of the world where there are no tornados, much less tornado alert systems, you'll hear the sound and see people scurrying around, you may even feel frightened, but you'll have no specific idea about the meaning of the sound.

Or if you're in a crowded building and you hear someone yell *fire!* most of you will know the meaning of this sound and you'll get out of the building immediately. But if you're from another country and speak no English, this sound has no meaning. It would be like hearing someone yell *X!*

You don't know what this sound is for. It has no meaning for you because you don't understand its intended purpose. You'll need to extract meaning as best you can by reading the expressions on people's faces and observing their actions.

To say something has meaning suggests it has a purpose. As you read a newspaper, or listen to debate, or study the scriptures, in order to understand the meanings ask yourself, "What do they want from their audience?"

Understanding their purpose will help you better grasp their meaning.

The tornado siren and someone yelling *fire!* in a building all have meanings because they're connected to a purpose. The sounds want the hearer to *do* something.

We have examples of the connection between sounds and purpose from popular culture. The four musical tones in Close Encounters of the Third Kind served as a message, a calling, to those elect few to meet the extraterrestrials on the mountain. In Star Trek IV: The Voyage Home the whale cry served as a cry for help.

Sounds have meaning when they have purpose.

The Gospel of John begins with these words, "In the beginning was the word and the word was with God and the word was God."

John continues a little later into the chapter: "And the word became flesh and dwelt among us."

The "word" becoming "flesh" is a way of talking about Jesus. Jesus is the sound God made. And because the one who made the sound has an intention for it, it's a word. A "word" is a sound that has purpose.

It's up to us, as listeners, to seek to understand the meaning of this sound. John tells us his take on it: "And the Word became flesh and lived among us, and we have seen his glory, the glory as of a father's only son, full of grace and truth."(John 1.14)

For many of us these words are just sounds. As an immigrant who learned English as his second language, I can tell you that listening to people speak a foreign language is like listening to gibberish. It's nothing but sounds. But after a painful while, these sounds became words.

The second task of leading from the future is to discern the meaning, the purpose, of the sounds within the chaos and then turn them into words others can understand.

*****

My need for air was beyond desperate. I had already missed breathing on two attempts. Panic was knocking at the door. As I approached the next wave, I knew I needed to get this thing right. This would be my last chance. I waited for the right moment when my ascent on the third wave reached its zenith. Then, at just the right split second, I extended my head as high as possible, opened my mouth widely, and inhaled in absolute need. It was really more a desperate gasp for air. And all I got was water. I was drowning.

Chapter 15

The First Futurist

For our ancient ancestors, the future was cemented in the stars. The fate of a person or a nation could not be changed anymore than the stars could be rearranged. The human imagination was ruled by the Celestial Sphere, the movement of planets and lights set within the ceiling of the heavens.

Their experience of time was cyclical. Grounded firmly in the seasons, with a time to reap and a time to sow, the human experience was a wheel. The future was a predictable return of the same. It was forever a return of the past. Meaning in life came by accepting one's destiny, one's place in the circle of life.

Until the change.

If Abraham were alive today, we'd known him as an Iraqi. But in the ancient world, the world before our modern Nation States, he was from the bustling waterfront town of Ur. He was a clever and prosperous chieftain in his time. Still he felt there was more left for him to do, a greater contribution he needed to make. But life was a wheel and he a mere spoke within it.

And then again, there were the voices. His guiding spirit had already called him to leave his country. "*Leave your country, your people and your father's household and go to the land I will show you,*" the spirit whispered. (Genesis 12.1)

And, one night, as he gazed upon the stars, the whispers came again: "'*Look up at the sky and count the stars—if indeed you can count them.*' Then the spirit said to him, '*So shall your offspring be.*'" (Genesis 15.5)

As the Father of Judaism, Christianity, and Islam, Abraham is a familiar figure to many. But in order to appreciate him we must detach him from our modern world. We must press even further and distance him from the ancient world. We must travel further back in time to a more primal world, an aboriginal world, a world before writing, before time as we know it. In that world, there was no history or futurity.

In that world, the present was a continuous return of the past.

Time and eternity, the earthly and the heavenly, were understood as a cycle in the world of Abraham's day. Time was measured less in any linear way, by clock time, and more by the recurring circular realities of winters (years), moons (months), and sleeps (days).

This understanding of time set the scene for Abraham's novel idea.

He was an old man of 75 with no heir. Nothing could change that. Nothing could change his future. To think otherwise was laughable. He could only find peace if he accepted his fate, accepted the wheel.

But, prompted by the guiding spirit that had taken an interest in him, he looked at the stars and dared to believe that, rather than a return of the expected, the future could bring something novel, something unexpected.

The first exchanges between Abraham and his guiding spirit must have been like the dickering of a clever, market smart tribal chieftain with a local deity. But with time, Abraham develops a relationship with the god behind the whispers.

His guiding spirit called him to leave what he knew for an unknown place, and the spirit was as clever a negotiator as was Abraham.

So Abraham set out into the unknown and in doing so, he invented the future.

The future as something other than the acceptance of an eternal return of the same, that is. Abraham broke the wheel. He initiates an epic adventure that would lead to monotheism, the people of Israel, Christianity, Islam, and, in the end, Western Culture.

The ancients saw time as a circle. Western Culture understands time as a line. They counted the return of winters. We bid the passing years adieu, never to be experienced again.

But perhaps time is neither a line nor a circle but a swirling pathway, a vortex, that spins around and around as it moves forward. The gift of Abraham to us was to demonstrate that the human story doesn't have to repeat itself, it can go somewhere.

He became the world's first futurist. Not an academic futurist. An action-oriented futurist who dared to pursue the future he preferred.

The Christian religion and the biblical literature, that both emerged in his wake, are not the future his story pointed towards. Instead they are signposts pointing beyond themselves in the same direction as Abraham: to the open possibilities of tomorrow.

Abraham's story introduces key concepts about the future. Against common sense, Abraham leaves the land he knows for a land he does not know. Rather than looking at the stars and seeing his future fate, he uses his imagination to rearrange their meaning.

This is a future sensibility. He trades certainty for possibility, fate for faith.

Unlike Abraham, most of us haven't heard disembodied voices. But many of us have had an insight, or an epiphany, or an idea, or even a gut feeling, which required courage to act upon. It took courage for Abraham to exchange everything he knew to be true for something even more true. He gambled that the wheel of fate could be escaped. He developed another future sensibility. Abraham developed hope.

Even secular futurists must have faith and hope. These sensibilities speak of a longing for a better tomorrow. Much of our thinking about the future is dystopian

106

and there's good reason for that. We know our history, ourselves, and each other all too well.

But, without faith and hope, why think about the future at all? Why create scenarios of alternative possibilities? Why warn others about possible dangers if not in the faith and hope that we could choose a different and better future?

Abraham's shift had far reaching implications. If he could break free of his place and his fate, then perhaps everything else about his world was up for grabs. Was his social world nothing more than a work of human design, a temporary condition enforced by those with the will to do so?

In the end, Abraham's creativity would permit us to see life as a journey. If the ancient view was cyclical, Abraham's new vision was forward. He discerned new meaning in the same stars, and everything changed for him and for us.

Abraham set out in faith and hopes of creating a different future for himself, a preferred future. He embodied the spirit of the words spoken by spanish poet Antonio Machado: "We make the path by walking."

*****

The first occurrence of the word love in the Bible occurs in Abraham's story. He loves his son Isaac. The whispers promised him, a man with no heir, a son. Abraham's dreams and hopes were bound to him. Abraham saw his future through his son Isaac.

Perhaps the first human experiences of love for children, as we experience it today, accompanied the emergent sensibilities of faith and hope?

We also begin to see in the relationship between Abraham and his guiding spirit signs of a dynamic relationship. Abraham and God haggle. As a result, rather than predictions based on the stars, we have promises based on relationship. Rather than a closed destiny, we have an open future of possibility.

Knowledge of a static future is replaced by interaction in an open system. Abraham's vision of the universe began to change. No longer a closed existence in which one's fate must simply be accepted, life became an open and dynamic experience filled with possibilities that must be pursued.

Meaning for the ancients came from accepting their place in the cycle. For Abraham, meaning was discovered in embracing a better future and pursuing it. As he pursued this new future, he began to write a new narrative.

His was a story that was going somewhere.

Our sense of meaning in life is birthed in Abraham's journey. First, meaning in life is birthed at the intersection where our experiences with the people and things we love meets our hopes and dreams of a different and better tomorrow. We feel joy when we imagine our children whom we love having wonderful future lives better than our own.

Second, we feel hope when we discover that the story we are in is open to possible new story lines.

Third, we are inspired to act in faith when we discover that we can be the authors of our new story lines and even of the roles we'll play in the story.

Abraham, the first futurist, taught us that we can change the script.

Chapter 16

Once Upon a Time

I stepped out onto the front porch of our home on the green side of the volcano. Many years before, when the Volcano of San Salvador had erupted, it didn't blow up through the top of the cone. Instead, the volcano exploded out of the side. Our side of the volcano became the "green side," an inhabited green landscape. The other side was a long and wide swath of hardened lava.

It was a brisk morning and I looked down the steps to the green Chevrolet parked on the sloping curb below.

My grandmother put her hand on my shoulder. "Are you happy?"

Instinctively, I grabbed the wrought-iron bars that protected our windows.

She pulled on my arm gently. "You'll be happy there. It's good."

I pulled myself toward the bars.

She struggled to pull me toward the car, but I squeezed the bars even more tightly.

My grandfather glanced at our tug of war as he walked past with the luggage.

My mother had taken a job as a flight attendant with the new Pan American Airlines and my younger brother, Erwin, and I had stayed behind living with our grandparents. After a year of training in Miami, then a year based in San Francisco, followed by a year based in New York, she finally settled in Miami and sent for us.

My grandfather placed the small suitcase into the trunk of the green Chevy and turned back to help loosen my grip on the fence.

Inevitably, the will of a defiant six-year-old submitted to the power of the way things had to be. And we moved to the States.

I understand how hard it is to let go.

*****

There's a lot of current research that demonstrates how and why "stories" are an effective way of communicating. Propositions may clarify things, but stories allow for complexity and interpretation, just like reality.

Jesus is known as a master story teller, but I don't think his stories were his way of dispensing wisdom for living a better life. He lived his life as if on an urgent mission. He was aware of the signs of his time. He anticipated a possible future that would bring the world as he and his kinsman knew it to an end. Because of this, his stories had an edge to them. And that's why Jesus had a lot to say about letting go.

He told those who hoped for Israel's political redemption that they should let go. He told the wealthy that they'd be better off letting go. He told those who were certain of their own righteousness to let go.

Some of his compatriots believed that God would come and defeat the Romans. God would then rule the world from Jerusalem. They lived out this story by antagonizing Roman rule. They were zealots and insurrectionists. They hung on to the hope of a political and military victory.

Others felt the best strategy was to play along. They accommodated themselves to Roman rule and sought to ingratiate themselves to those in power. They didn't want to rock the boat. The held on to the status quo.

Both of these narratives were bound to their land.

In contrast, Jesus anticipated a different future. He imagined the fall of their beloved Temple in Jerusalem and the annihilation of Israel.

They faced an extinction event.

Jesus' goal wasn't to save the established order. He wasn't on the side of accommodation. Neither was his goal to overthrow the established order. He wasn't on the side of the rebels.

He called them all to let go of their dreams, their hopes. The kingdom that he represented came in judgement of the world. None of it worked.

To survive extinction, he rewrote the story. This is why he had been sent, not to condemn for his world was condemned already, but to provide a way through and out. He called out and created an alternative community that would escape through a narrow way that would be carved within the tribulations of those days and survive to evolve.

•••••

Sometimes we can mistake an artifact for the meaning behind it. Whether it be the tradition of the Temple in Jerusalem, the Latin Mass, the Papacy, the Bible, the color of the church carpet, the style of music in worship, or the number of attenders on Sunday, we often tend to cling to the wrong things.

But we live in a time of such rapid change, clinging to the wrong things mean disappearing along with them into the dark sea of the past. To get past the disruptive changes of the present, we'll need to search our stories for clues that tell us what to let go and what to bring forward.

But for many today, the old stories that gave our lives meaning no longer work. By old stories here I don't mean our myths and legends. I mean our histories.

Take the story of the American genesis. There are many inspiring and unique aspects about the origins of the United States. The world may indeed be better off because the United States exists and occupies such a prominent place in the global arena.

But the story of the American genesis is differently told by the First Nations — the native peoples of North America. The meaning a story conveys depends on the point of view of the story teller.

Or take the America as described by the conservative narrative. Some conservatives seem to long for a return to the idyllic small town life of Mayberry R.F.D. This narrative points to a time when the nation was still innocent. The story they tell sees the world from the perspective of the status quo. But would they long to return to the south in the '50s and '60s if they were black, gay, or female?

The description "innocent" does capture a slice of that world. There are "innocent" aspects that many of us — white, black, male, female, straight and gay — would desire for our children. A world of relaxed humor, bare feet and fishing poles, a less-sexualized and less violent world in a modest friendly small town. Mayberry's deputy sheriff, in fact, has a gun but no bullets because they're simply not needed and might hurt someone.

But, just like Mayberry, that world is a fiction. Few of us would want to rewind the progress we've made in the place of women, accepting cultural diversity as good, of expanding the circle of who we call "us," and of rejecting violent prejudice.

In the fictional world of Mayberry, crime came only with visitors from the outside, strangers. But we are coming to understand that the problems we face cannot be blamed on *them*, the outsiders, the strangers. The source of the problems can be found much closer to home.

On the other hand, some progressives seem to long for a world of unbounded freedom. In their preferred future, people are finally set free from traditional institutions and perceptions, free to experiment and do what each individually want.

These forces of disintegration are embedded within our institutions. For example, progressives benefit when women remain unmarried, whether or not they have children, because women who marry tend to vote more regularly for conservatives. Because the political drive to remain in power supersedes the drive to work for the good of the country, progressives will champion the forces that bring them more votes.

They will champion "freedom" unless, that is, it contradicts the progressive point of view. Those who do contradict their point of view are not exercising freedom. They are regarded as backwards, bigots, phobic, etc.

Like Mayberry, this world is also a fiction. Few of us would want to send our children into a future in which moral good was governed by individual preference. This future is a world without virtue, without discipline, without innocence. It is, ultimately, a world without freedom.

Overall, whether conservative or progressive, we're all more sensitive about the stories we hear and tell. We know that stories are slanted in the direction of the story tellers.

That's why apologies are so important to humans. Apologies are stories in which the teller isn't the good guy. They are attempts to bring integrity to all the characters involved in the narrative. It's a story in which we let go of our defenses and make ourselves vulnerable for the sake of the relationship.

We're beginning to understand that history, the way we tell it, is only a perspective of history. It's a story with a point of view.

Even the stories of faith no longer hold the culture together. Faith narratives that incorporate necessary new knowledge have yet to be created.

For example, the history of life on Earth includes millions of years of pain and suffering in the natural world before the emergence of man. This creates problems for those who read the Genesis story chronologically, even though the book of Job includes predators (and thus predation) as a part of God's original design.

In their reading, life was perfect, harmonious, and peaceful, until mankind "fell" due to the betrayal in the Garden of Eden. Then sin and all of its consequences entered the world. So, according to this reading, there could not have been suffering before the "fall."

Another example would be familial structures. Recent studies in DNA demonstrate that polygyny, one man and multiple women, was a likely familial structure among early humans. This might create problems for those who understand, through their reading of Genesis, that the original family structure was one man and one woman. Then after the "fall" the family structure deteriorated from there to other types of arrangements.

But even the stories of Abraham, who embraced a concubine as a surrogate mother, and David, who had several wives, in the Old Testament demonstrate a certain flexibility in understanding marital arrangements.

The scriptures need to be reengaged and reframed in light of new knowledge… without falling into the trap of arrogantly believing that we're the first generation to know anything.

In the social domains, rather than reading the scriptures as a narrative that turns power upside down and the world inside out, our religious institutions often serve to maintain the status quo.

The same story of faith when told by the slave, the poor, the revolutionary, and the marginalized can carry different meanings than when told by the plantation owner, the powerful, the dictator, or those who are deeply invested in the power structures.

Orthodoxy may be little more than the heresy that won, and we are becoming more sensitive to the voices of the defeated.

Jesus consolidated, upgraded, and amplified our ability to hear the oppressed. He shattered expectations by touching lepers, talking to women, helping gentiles, healing on the Sabbath, and dining with sinners.

He introduced his world to a new way of becoming human.

The early disciples that embraced Jesus' way of becoming human became the community of the spirit of Christ. And the community of the spirit did survive the destruction of the Temple in the seventh decade. And they understood that the greater point of the life of Jesus was not the stories he told, but Jesus himself.

He embodied the history and futurity of the human story. He was an advocate for the first century outsiders of society, whether they be poor, leprous, diseased, gentiles, or women. God, Jesus insisted, is with them. And God is with us, he warned his compatriots, as long as we are with them too.

What kind of story is this?

It's a story that invites us to let go. This kind of message knocks all of us who have something to lose back on our heels. For those in power and with place, no good could come of this kind of teaching.

If we were to approach the Bible in the same way that Etsuru Sotoo approached La Sagrada Familia, looking through the Bible rather than looking at it, what would we see? Where is Jesus' God taking the human story? What is the future trajectory of slavery, marriage, immigration, sexuality, nations, economics, politics, technology, war, the role of women, and the marginalized?

Engaging this question will mean learning that there are things- sacred things, material things, social things, emotional things- which we must find the courage to let go.

As I think about our age of rapid change, I wonder, is the movement of Jesus in Western Culture facing an extinction event at the beginning of the 21st century? Probably not. The spirit of Christ continues to call out followers of the way. But the church as an institution might be because western culture itself may be facing an extinction event.

115

If it is, the church must let go of power and place and prestige or die. Makers of fire, entrepreneurs of the spirit, are those who, if and when the world goes dark, will know how to make fire again. And, as it was for the first century communities of the spirit, so it will be for twenty-first century communities of the spirit: the way of salvation may be narrow.

The apostles Peter and Paul took things further. Everywhere they announced the story of Jesus, new communities of the spirit emerged in which the barriers between Jew and gentile, slave and free, rich and poor, male and female were brought down and their roles set on new trajectories. This community of the spirit was to be a signpost of the future.

Have the communities of the spirit always done this?

No.

But the stories are embedded in their history and in their scripture as trajectories for the future.

This oxygen of meaning nurtured the fires of change in first-century Jerusalem. God has opened his table to the sinner, the powerless, the outsider, and the marginalized, and the movement spread throughout the Roman Empire. We can anticipate at least two possible futures as this message clashed with Rome.

In one future the Emperor and the Roman Senate would hear the message, fall in love with its grace and truth, repent of the ways they exploited the peoples and nations around them, freely give of their own wealth to the poor, and use all of their power to ease suffering. In other words, they could let go. They could fall on their faces and worship a god like this one.

Another future might be that they would choose to cling to what they knew. They could defend the gods that sanctioned their place, power, and prestige in the world. They might decide to stamp out such a destabilizing and irresponsible message and denounce its pitiful god who died nailed to a post.

And once upon a time, followers of Jesus were inhumanely executed by the Romans. And no matter how hard Rome tried to snuff out the smoldering ashes of this new faith, the embers of the communities of the spirit continued to start new fires. Eventually some three hundred years later, when it served the Roman self interest under the rule of the Emperor Constantine, the Romans chose to tolerate Christianity. Finally, as noted by scholar FF Bruce in his work on the apostle Paul, a world that once named their sons after the Emperors, and their dogs after Christ's disciples, became a world that named their sons Paul and their dogs Nero.

That's the power of a story.

According to the scriptures, God is on a mission to eradicate xenophobia from the face of the Earth. Xenophobia is the fear of strangers.

This story line begins with Abraham, continues in the prophets, is confirmed by Jesus, and called out by the spirt in the church.

In Genesis 12 when Abraham is approached by his guiding spirit, they make an agreement.

"I will make you into a great nation and I will bless you; I will make your name great, and you will be a blessing. I will bless those who bless you, and whoever curses you I will curse; and all peoples on earth will be blessed through you."

Through this relationship, "all peoples on earth will be blessed."

All peoples. Extraordinary.

Thousands of years before social media, this guiding spirit and Abraham set out to "friend" the whole Earth.

This is a future trajectory that is shaping the world. The prophets and the psalmists also offer a ray of light for the nations.

May God be gracious to us and bless us and make his face shine   o   n us— so that your ways may be known on earth, your salvation a m o n g   a l l nations. (Psalm 67)

Jesus builds on this story line. He tells his disciples after his resurrection, "*Go and make disciples of all nations.*"

This story is one of inclusion, of growing circles of concern, of blessing all the families of the Earth. It's a journey from xenophobia, the fear of strangers, towards xenophilia, the love of strangers.

It's a journey from The Wheel that asserts the world will always be violent, always be oppressive, always be full of hate for the "other," to a Vortex moving towards a future that is open to surprise, to novelty, to something beautiful.

This journey from fear to love is the story we're in. It carries within it the meaning of and the secrets to becoming human.

The stories we tell matter, because virtue-and-values-shaping culture rises out of narratives.

Viking culture rose out of their Norse myths and their experience as a seafaring people from the rugged top of the world.

Jewish culture rose out of their stories of redemption in the Hebrew scriptures and their journey from Egypt to Israel.

American culture rises out of the pioneering, liberty-seeking, and risk-taking character of the peoples who populated North America and the narratives of the American genesis.

This is why the stories of the Creation, Cain and Abel, Abraham, Jesus, and the early church are important to tell. These are the stories of the journey to become human. And, in the end, our lives and our cultures are nothing more than stories. In the words of feminist poet Muriel Rukeyser, "The universe is made of stories, not atoms."

*****

I was drowning. And I knew it. I had already missed three opportunities to breathe.

In desperation I turned around and faced upstream towards my raft. This meant I was floating downstream back first. That's a dangerous idea in fast moving water.

I waved my hand above my head in the universal sign for help.

That sign has meaning because it has purpose. It tells a story: I'm in trouble. Help.

In a few seconds the crew drew the raft within reach and one of the team extended an oar. I grabbed it and they pulled me alongside. They immediately grabbed my personal flotation device and pulled me over the side and into the raft. I didn't notice that from the moment I turned around in the water, without even realizing it, I was already breathing.

My son Michael so relaxed and cool as always smiled at me. "Dad, what happened?"

From their perspective the whole episode lasted less than two minutes. The back of my head had been visible to them the whole time. From their perspective, I should have been able to access as much Oxygen as I needed. And yet, I had almost drowned while floating above water.

What happened in those one hundred and twenty seconds all depends on how you look at it.

Chapter 17

Blue Moments

We were rolling through a crowded intersection near downtown San Salvador. My grandfather was at the wheel of his green Chevrolet and the sounds of the street—horns honking, vendors hawking their wares, the occasional bleating of a goat—poured in through the open windows. Women in traditional garb slapped dough in their hands to make pupusas, a kind of thick flour tortilla stuffed with cheese, *loroco* (a native herb), and pork—the smoke and smell of it all filled the air. In the midst of all of this, beggars lined the road, one with deformed legs below the knee, another with a huge goiter on the neck the size of half a head, another missing a limb.

My grandfather was resting his arm on the door of the car. As our car slowed, he brought his arm inside. "You can't show your watch here, Alexito," he said. "Someone will walk right up and tear it off."

I looked past him into the street and watched a boy step out from the blurry mass of pedestrian traffic. He was a skinny, shirtless kid about my age with dark hair and brown eyes. He approached our car and begged for money.

My grandfather glanced at the boy. "Where's your father?"

"Dead," said the boy.

"Your father's at home, drunk."

"No. He died," the boy answered.

Our car inched forward and I turned my head and watched the boy walk away. Before he melded into the moving crowd, he looked back over his shoulder and caught my eyes. In that moment, as our eyes met, everything around me was blocked out. No sounds. No heat. No time. I didn't fully grasp it then, but that moment of eye contact between us was what I call a blue moment.

I call these blue moments because they are like hyperlinks on a computer screen. On our computers most of the text appears black—whether on simple word processing documents or interactive web pages. But sometimes a word or a phrase is bright blue. This indicates a hyperlink. Unlike the rest, this text is pregnant with embedded information that, when clicked, will lead to more. Much more.

Like hyperlinks, blue moments are experiences pregnant with unseen meaning that beckon us to press into them. Blue moments open windows of insight into what it means to be human, and they call upon us to do something— to follow them.

Over time I discovered that I am one of many, many people who have these kinds of experiences. But it's not just our experiences that lead us along the path of becoming human. It's also the way our brains are wired.

Wired

Neuroscience researcher Matthew Lieberman tells us that social pain affects the same parts of the brain as physical pain. In other words, the pain we feel when separated from a loved one isn't just figurative or metaphorical. It is real pain. He claims, "our urge to connect and the pain we feel when this need is thwarted is one of the seminal achievements of the human brain."

Our brain is evolving according to the narrative arc described in the scriptures. In the same way that human technology is on mission with God to reconnect the world, God's technology, the human brain, is on mission with God too.

The ancients, before neuroscience, understood that being disconnected hurts. They discovered that creating connections would heal the hurt. They scripted a change in behavior into the human narrative. They included in their tribal lore instructions for the care of strangers and foreigners among their people.

I often wonder if their laws reflected a line of thinking that was sweeping across the ancient world. Or were they unique signposts of the future? Either way, the hebrews either had great powers of observation or amazing powers of anticipation and imagination.

Today we know that it's not just our interpersonal connections that are broken; it's also our grasp of the world around us. In our experiences, we know disease, but fail to understand health. We know death, but wonder if we will ever truly live. We have an inner sense that everything is going to be all right but have no evidence to think that. Our lives seem to point to something more, to some beautiful mystery, but our links are broken.

Religion alerts us to our broken connections and wrestles with the reality of human fragmentation. In concert with religion, the healing sciences—therapy, medicine, counseling—also speak of human dysfunction and disease and seek to alleviate personal pain and interpersonal alienation. To heal the broken links in our world, Buddhism invites us to journey toward enlightenment and seek a way beyond suffering. Scientism urges us to grasp empirical facts and observable evidence. Christianity and Judaism both take human fragmentation seriously and offer a way to atone for guilt and sin, and Hinduism speaks of the human condition as delusion. It's essential that humankind be enlightened, informed, and made whole, but in order to heal our world, we will have to do more than that. We will have to become human.

Westerners tend to see the ideal human as an autonomous individual. This solitary individual bravely makes his or her own "independent" choices. The west is a "pro-individual-choice" culture. Knowledge and wisdom are understood to reside within the individual power of reason and the individual is often prioritized over the community.

Western individualism highlights the value and importance of the person. This is an immense contribution to the world. This flies in the face of empires. We are not faceless beings that meld into the crowd. We are persons without which the community could not exist, for it is comprised of persons. We each have a face.

But each of us could not exist without community.

The biblical narrative sees humanity differently. The ideal human isn't an autonomous, solitary, independent individual making his or her way bravely in the world. The ideal human isn't a human being but a human connecting.

Humanity is designed for community. But community isn't the same thing as a crowd or a collective. Collectives can suppress the individual into nonexistence. The crowd is one extreme towards which 21st century technology is pushing us. The crowd is faceless and anonymous and ubiquitous. Have you ever had an anonymous comment on your blog or social network? That's the crowd, the faceless collective.

In community each person is known. Every person has a personal name and is responsible for their actions and celebrated for their uniqueness. This embrace of a person's uniqueness is what makes a community trustworthy.

In the same way, every person recognizes their need for their tribe or community and offers themselves in service. This commitment is what allows community to delight in the uniqueness of personal genius.

The meaning of being human, of being a person, only begins to take shape when we recognize both our personal responsibility and profound connection to each other.

Of course, our interconnection is often denied. Recently I heard a proverb from India: "The tears of a stranger are only water." The implication is that strangers don't have value. This depreciation of strangers points to a profound disconnection at the heart level. This disconnection isn't unique to South Asians. It has expression in ethnic, cultural, or class-based hatred in all cultures of which I am aware. To say we *can* become human does not mean that we all *will* become human. We can choose an inhumane path. We can choose to distort the most fundamental of truths, the truth that we are all connected.

*****

The Bible opens with a poetic saga, a poem of creation, that places relationships at the heart of the cosmic story. The story suggests that meaning in the world is found in relationships, not in things. We might say, that, while God's fingerprint is everywhere in the universe, meaning in life will not be found by simply studying the materials (the "what") that make up the universe. Nor will meaning be found in the mechanics (the "how") that describe the processes by which life evolved or is experienced. Meaning is found in the personal, relational, and communal through the future-oriented capacities of faith and hope.

The biblical story reflects our world in which relationships are broken, in which neighbor hates neighbor. And surprisingly, even though the Hebrews lived in a world that was every bit as fearful of strangers as ours, their Scriptures suggested a different kind of possible future.

When foreigners reside among you in your land, do not mistreat them. The foreigners residing among you must be treated as your native-born. Love them as yourself, for you were foreigners in Egypt. I am the Lord your God.

Did Israelites always live up to this mandate to love foreigners?

No.

But the cultural resource for evolving to the next iteration of relationships was embedded into their experience, history, and scripture.

If meaning is discovered personally, relationally, and communally, then meaning in life is experienced (and discovered) in personally "living out" a narrative in relationship to a community that seeks to heal the world and reconcile all peoples. We discover meaning when we do this because we align ourselves with the work, according to the scripture, of God.

Because of the continuity between the Hebrew experience of faith and the faith of the early Christians, this value was passed from the Hebrew Scriptures into the New Testament. There it is expressed with the word "hospitality." Hospitality in the language of the New Testament is the combination of two words, "stranger" and "love," and means literally "the love of strangers."

Hospitality is the nemesis of xenophobia.

In the vision of the New Testament, the home is the hub for creating a world with no strangers. This is a picture of how, in the biblical imagination, God deals with humankind. He opens his heart and home and invites us to sit at his table and share a meal.

In the world of the wheel, animosity will return again and again, for the future isn't anything more than the return of the past.

There seems to be so much truth in this.

125

In the biblical imagination, a future in which we inhabit Earth as one global family is an open possibility. But we will have to break with the wheel. We will need to leave one truth for something even more true.

God, according to the scriptures, is on a quest to end our alienation, to reconcile our irreconcilable differences. He is on a mission to eradicate xenophobia—the fear of strangers—from humanity. We join God's mission when we choose to befriend the world.

Abraham's encounter with God is a crucial plot point in the human story. He doesn't want anyone to be a "them." He wants everyone to be an "us."

This mission is still in the beginning stages, and it pivots on what I call the Human Event: the life, death, and resurrection of Jesus. How is Jesus relevant to our 21st Century world in which accelerating technology, global competition, and shifting demographics and social norms are morphing our societies and ways of life?

In terms of accelerating technology and global competition we are to serve and treat our global competitors as one of our own loved ones. In terms of the shifting demographics and social norms that are changing our neighborhoods and cities, we are to love our neighbors as ourselves. In terms of immigrants at our borders, we are to love our neighbors children as our own children. Nothing could be more relevant in our connectivity-rich, community-starved world. No one's leadership and wisdom speaks more to the moment than Jesus of Nazareth.

Chapter 18

The Air We Breathe

In order to start a fire, you'll need a flow of oxygenating air.

In our triangle of combustion, Fuel is the world around us, the world we have received. It's the "what."

The Heat of Ignition is the person or community that brings the spark of creativity. It's the "how."

And Oxygen is the invisible life-giving quality, the meaning and purpose we attribute to things. It's the "why."

I read a story once about the last people on the last habitable planet warmed by the last star in the universe. These last people had lived billions of years moving from star system to star system and, as the universe wound to a close, they were happy it was finally over. They were tired of fleeing and relieved to reach the end of all things. No grand purpose or scheme. Just the flicker of last light, then dark.

This story works because it touches the deepest fiber of what it means to be human. We long for a sense of meaning. Without it, we flicker and die like a flame in a vacuum, no more meaningful or meaningless than the faltering stars we contemplate. As fire needs oxygen to burn, we seek meaning to live.

Some people find it impossible to believe that life has meaning. But some things are so important for a healthy society, so significant for the human experience, that they are worth pursuing even when they seem impossible to reach. Even those who have given up on discovering any ultimate meaning in life take on the important task of inventing it.

Some use the language of objective and subjective to make this distinction between discovered and invented meaning. Something objective exists in and of itself, with or without us. It's out there waiting to be discovered.

You've heard the question, if a tree falls in the forest and there is no one there to hear it, does it still make a sound? The pure subjectivist would say there is no tree and no forest unless we're there to perceive it. An objectivist would say that if a tree fell in the forest, then it fell even if we weren't there to subjectively perceive it.

We cannot escape our subjectivity. But one acknowledges the objective reality around us. The other does not.

In the same way, some believe that meaning has an objective reality. They believe that there is something greater than ourselves that gives our experience meaning. It exists whether or not we perceive it.

Others say, there is no meaning except that which we create.

Whether discovered or invented, we are meaning-seeking creatures.

But we live such hurried lives. An entire lifetime may come and go before we turn to the important questions. It sometimes seems that the only people who stop and take stock of their lives, the world and the beauty in it, are those people who receive a horrifying diagnosis and face their ultimate battles.

Why do we wait for that dreaded diagnosis? Perhaps it's because, while our culture is drowning in data, it cannot breathe for lack of wisdom. The Psalmist wrote: "*learn to number your days that you may gain a heart of wisdom.*"

Paying attention to the transitoriness of our lives now can nurture wisdom.

It can also nurture despair.

The pursuit of an ultimate and objective meaning embraces that, although it's subjectively perceived, Meaning comes to us from the outside. All human cultures and most people who have ever lived have understood life this way. Meaning exists as an objective reality –grounded in the aether, in God, the gods, our myths, the spirits, or the universe– and our task is to discover it.

Some humanists suggest an alternative way. Find a sense of meaning, they suggest, in your life, your loves, your family, in the world. Meaning comes from our temporal commitments. I have a deep sympathy and resonance to this point of view. It was my own before I was surprised by faith.

For humanists, whatever meaning there is exists only in the transient sensory experiences we have now. And when our loved ones are gone, they are returned to nothing. As for the world, it will all come to an end for you, the day you do. Beyond this there is nothing.

This is painful. And, at first, it seems courageous. This makes sense, if you have no other path. It's a stiff upper lip approach. This is what reality is. Let's deal with it.

To accept this as truth may lead some to despair. But the majority of atheists and humanists do not jump off bridges. I don't think it's because of some great courage in face of the great abyss. I think it's due to two factors. First, this truth requires an anesthetic to dull the senses. One way to dull the senses is by *inventing* meaning. Second, we don't jump off bridges because something within us —within all of us— resists giving in to despair.

I take the stories of scripture to indicate that invented meaning works precisely because (and when) it aligns to the true undercurrents of meaning that support reality. Something within us "knows" there is more to life than we now know.

Believing is about waking up to this knowledge while acknowledging its limits.

Rather than an anesthetic to dull the senses, the view of faith requires an esthetic. An esthetic primes and sharpens the senses.

This approach is even more painful than the anesthetic approach. It embraces the doubt we all have. But it also embraces hope. This opens the heart to even more pain. It opens us to heartbreak. It opens us to the possibility of becoming human.

People who can't believe might consider one thing. Perhaps such certainty about the meaninglessness of it all is premature. Not only do we know so little about our universe as it is and ourselves as we are, but the world is still blossoming, still unfolding, still being created. Who knows what surprising and beautiful things remain to be discovered? Why be in such a rush to judgment rather than stay open?

It's true that this openness may prove too painful. Only faith, hope, and love can survive such pain.

Just to be clear, both a commitment to invented or discovered meaning demand a personal surrender in the face of unknowing. And they both alike refuse to accept the vacuum of meaninglessness. Hand in hand they together gasp for air. One gasps in hope and the other without hope. That's how important it is for us to believe, to have meaning. We discover it. We invent it. We pursue it. We suppress it. We cannot escape our need for it. It's the air we breathe. It's oxygen.

In the 21st century, we urban-animals, secular-but-spiritual selves, post-modern modernists, post-human primates, scientifically enlightened and yet somehow less-rational-than-ever creatures, still need Meaning.

Chapter 19

What Does it Mean to be Human?

Glen stretched out the microphone towards the kill. The squeals of the prey animal trying to breathe as the lion clamped down on its throat would haunt him.

Glen was the sound guy on a South African expedition to document a lion pride during a hunt. In order to capture the best possible sound, he was perched in a "nest" on the end of a boom extending in front of the vehicle. His job was to extend the microphone as close to the action as possible. The film crew successfully filmed a kill and Glen witnessed the whole event up close from his perch.

As he detailed his experience to me, he repeated that what he most remembered were the sounds.

What does this have to do with what it means to be human?

In light of the lion kill, think about the uniqueness of this word: *inhumane*.

Inhumane means not humanlike, not human. This is unique.

We don't watch a lion take down a prey animal and say, "how inleonine, not lion-like, *not lion*." It's perfectly in character for a lion to do such a thing. The lion is merely acting according to his nature.

In fact, we don't have common terms that express the negation of other species' natures. Why? Because what they do conforms to what they are.

Why then do we have a common term that is a negation of ourselves?

We do say of ourselves: "How inhumane"?

We must ask, Is our "inhumanity" an expression of our nature or a contradiction of it? And if our "inhumanity" is a contradiction of our human nature, where did this idea come from?

Is our need to kill instinctual, the consequence of genetic evolution? Is it something we should remove if the possibility presents itself through genetic therapy? Is it possible to become a "non-killing global society"? What might be the unintended consequences?

Or, is the inclination to kill a cultural artifact, the product of memetic evolution? In other words, is it something we have learned by imitation? Is it something that can be unlearned?

Glen told me that hours after filming the kill, even after they had returned to camp, his hands were still trembling. Yet he never questioned the morality of the lion kill.

None of us do.

Predatory animals hunt and kill. We understand this as nature at work. It's at one and the same time both terrifying and marvelous. God's handiwork.

Why, then, do we hold the human animal to such a different standard? As we pursue the question, What does it mean to be human? it may help to ask, Why does the word 'inhumane' even exist?

I suggest the word "inhumane" is a sign that we are discovering a meaning to life. Our purpose is to reject inhumanity and build a civilization that is consumed by love. In other words, our purpose is to become human.

*****

We're learning to hack life at the genetic level, like we hack computers. We make clones. We create synthetic life forms. The biopunk movement encourages "wet hackers" to experiment with DIY genetic and technological enhancements. Google has made a "google drive for genomes." Soon anyone anywhere may be able to access the genetic information of any living thing.

132

Will we be able to hack the human genome and put an end to the inhumane? God could have stopped Cain from killing Abel. But he couldn't force Cain to love him. To force love is to erase love, for love must be freely given. God was powerless before Cain. Will we be able to do better?

But God didn't give up. The scriptures tell us that the reason God didn't set the heavens and the Earth on fire is because He loved His world. To quote one of the most famous verses of literature in the world, *"For God so loved the world that he sent his son..."* (John 3.16)

This is the undercurrent of meaning that undergirds the whole of the cosmos and the details of every single life.

Jesus was sent to realign the world towards God. He was goodness incarnate, but the system experienced him like a malignant cell. To protect itself it sought to kill him. As an act of love for God and the world, Jesus endures its attacks.

This appeals to the subjective aspects of our being. We are inspired by love.

But there are objective realities at play too.

So God hacks the universe through the resurrection of Jesus Christ.

It wasn't enough to reach into the human genome and make a change. The hack had to be made at a more fundamental level. God reached beyond the genome of every living thing to the intersection of the inanimate and the animate, to the place where life itself and death meet.

There God changes the script.

The Creator raises Jesus from the dead by love. And love becomes the glue that will hold the decomposing universe together.

*****

133

What's the greatest evidence for God? Ask people this question. They will say things like the Bible, the church, the Pope, or the complexity of nature. The scriptures say that the greatest evidence of God in the creation is humankind. We are made in his image.

This story is told in the opening chapters of Genesis. God creates humankind and gives them everything. Only one thing God withholds: the fruit from the tree of the knowledge of good and evil. He tells humans that if they eat from the tree they will die.

In private counsel, God discloses a different reason for withholding the one fruit. He forbids it because, if they eat it, they will become like him. They will know good and evil.

One interpretive reading focuses on what is called "the fall of man." This reading goes like this: God creates humankind. Humankind disobeys God. Humans become less than they were created to be. God executes a redemptive plan that culminates in Jesus to pick humans up from their fall and restore them to the fullness of their humanity.

A second reading looks through the filter of "growing up." When humans disobey God, they don't become *less* like God, rather, they become *more* like him in that they "know good and evil." They are not, however, ready to bear this knowledge. They are naïve and immature. And now they are traumatized. God executes a plan of maturation, culminating in Jesus as the perfect model of human maturity, to apprentice humans to wisely bear the burden of responsibility, mystery, and paradox.

A third possible reading may come from an evolutionary perspective. This reading says the "image of God" points to a not-yet-finished product, an ideal. God doesn't stop creating at the end of Genesis chapter one; the process is still ongoing. In other words, we are *still being created* and as we evolve so does the image of God.

This may require people of faith to look at the biblical narrative a different way. Rather than a one layered story of Israel, which it certainly is, that culminates when the Temple is destroyed in 70 AD, the biblical story opens another layer, the story of humanity.

This makes the whole of the Bible, from Genesis to Revelation, a creation story. The story begins with the Spirit of God hovering over the face of the deep, moves to the emergence of life on Earth, culminates in humankind who develops a moral sense accompanied by experiences with the darkness of evil and the beauty of love, reaches a turning point with the archetypal human Jesus through which God hacks the universe, reboots with the downloading of the Spirit into the minds of women and men, and continues to press toward the goal of the creation story, foreshadowed in the resurrection of Jesus Christ, millions or billions of years in the future, when we all become human. At that point the creation story will be complete. And then the story of the things beyond all things can finally begin.

Becoming Human

Every now and then I'll hear someone say, "We're not human *doings*, we're human *beings*." They try to emphasize our identity, the priority of who we are, over our works, the value of what we do.

However, this term *human being* doesn't sit well either. We don't have "being" in and of ourselves. We're not immortal or eternally existent. The term *human creature* is closer to the truth. Whether you're a theist or not, you recognize that humans had a beginning. Through an act of God or through evolutionary forces or both, we came into existence. We are creatures just like all the other life forms that populate our ecosystem.

Still, even *human creature* sticks a little. Emphasizing our creatureliness highlights the things we have in common with our nonhuman neighbors, but it cannot account for the blue moments, the nagging evidence that, while we are undeniably creatures, we are something more—or we ought to be.

We are also creators. And we are co-creators of the human story. What we will become is partly in our hands.

We are *human becomings*.

We are a story in the middle of the telling. There is great value in what we aspire to "be" *and* what we "do." Both are necessary for our "becoming."

So rejoice. God is indeed not yet finished with us. But his goal may not be to make us better Christians. Jesus did not come to make the world Christian. We can set our sights higher. He came to make the world human.

So, perhaps we humans are meant to become the "image of God." Our species as a whole is intended to reflect the character and do the work of God. The poem tells us,

> God blessed them and said to them, "Be fruitful and increase in number; fill the earth and subdue it. Rule over the fish in the sea and the birds in the sky and over every living creature that moves on the ground." (Genesis 1. 28)

How does God rule? He makes all things thrive. The thrust of this commission is species-wide, not individual, and the intended consequence is that humankind would make all things thrive.

In the New Testament, this changes. Rather than the human species reflecting the "image of God," God's character and God's work is focused on an individual person named Jesus.

Let's begin with a basic thought about his purpose. Again, Jesus did not want to make us Christian. This just isn't big enough. Jesus wants to make us human. He wants the world to thrive again.

When I describe the purpose of Jesus like this in casual conversation, it isn't unusual for someone to answer me, "No thanks. We're human enough."

In their mind, *human* means depraved, sinful, dirty, and evil. A quick survey of history makes this point of view understandable. That's not all that can be said about us, but it certainly can be said.

For many of us, being human is a problem, a flaw to overcome. *Human*, then, is synonymous with *sinner*. This version of the human story begins in chapter three of Genesis with the "fall" of Adam, but it seems to end there too. This deep self-hatred, a hatred of the *human*, is common in some sects of the Christian faith.

But the human story doesn't begin with chapter three of Genesis. We must also take into account chapters one and two. The first two chapters of Genesis are not a scientific rendering of the origins of the universe. They are an epic saga.

In it, God creates humankind *"in His Image."* This poem describes our dream state, the culmination of our journey. This is the image of an ideal: humanity at peace with self, others, nature, and God. It's a preferred future, a vision, a guiding light.

And God is hacking the universe towards this end.

The desire to become that which God intended — that is, human — would seem to fit well within the scope of the story. In the Genesis poem God says, "Let us make humankind in our image." Still, even though God states this as His goal, for many believers, being human is the problem. For many of these believers becoming Christian is the solution to being human. They read the scriptures as if God had said, "Let us make christian-kind in our image."

If chapters one and two of Genesis describe our *dream state*, chapter four, after the man and woman are exiled from the Garden of Eden into the wilderness (Genesis 3), describes our natural or experiential state. This is the world as we know it.

Along with the beauty of life, we also experience death, disease, discord, demonizations, and disasters. This is our *nightmare*. But the nightmare doesn't dispel the dream. They comprise the two wings of our existence.

In chapter four we are told the famous story of two brothers, Cain and Abel. Cain murders Abel and there arises the first question humankind asks of God. When God is searching for Abel, the murdered brother, he comes to Cain to inquire about him.

"Where is your brother Abel?"

"I don't know," Cain replied. "Am I my brother's keeper?"

(Genesis 4.9)

Human history itself is an attempt to answer that question.

Cain is most certainly *not* Abel's keeper. He is far, far more than that. He is Abel's brother. This isn't political rhetoric. It's biology. It is also religion. It is also human.

How to become human is a discovery that we are in the process of making. How we each enter this process varies. Some enter alone through an epiphany. Others enter as they work together in service to others. Still others enter when they experienced important life events like expecting a first child or a loved one dies.

We often experience this as self-understanding. Disciples of Jesus throughout the centuries have discovered that telling the story of Jesus helps many make this discovery.

The bad news is that there is within each of us "the inhumane" with which we must get in touch if we are to cast it out. The good news is that there is also within each of us, waiting to be discovered, the human path.

This is what Jesus was talking about when he said that He was the way. The human path isn't an impersonal way of detachment. It's a personal, relational, and communal way of connection. And Jesus is walking on this way with any who will join him.

To "be human", then, is an aspiration. It's an unfashionable teleo-narrative, a narrative with a meaning and purpose, a narrative that goes somewhere. So, instead of asking what it means to be human, it may be more helpful to ask, what will it take to become human?

*****

Wars come and go on the stage of human history. But one war persists: the battle for the human heart. This internal fight is between futurity, what we are becoming, the power of choice to shape us, and history, what we have been, the tenacity of our past to imprison us.

This embodiment of the dream state and the natural state describes the current mental stage of our evolution. What happens when a creature awakens to an unprecedented level of self-awareness, to increasingly powerful feelings of empathy, then finds itself brutally killing another not by instinct but by choice?

This is the Cain and Abel predicament we find ourselves in.

We cannot devolve to a prior state in order to escape our newly discovered moral sense. We must either live with it or try to find our way forward. The result of our predicament is a polarization between the dream state and the natural state, what we could call heavens and hells, dreams and nightmares, possibilities and actualities.

Finding our way forward is a spiritual process that requires faith in unseen possibilities, hope in the midst of struggle, and love for one another. Each of these is a highly evolved function.

Both faith and hope are future-oriented capacities that would be impossible without the evolved multi-chambered brain that gave rise to the human imagination. We construct futures, entire new universes, in our imaginations. Love is the emergent capacity of empathetically including others within our own self-identity. It's the context for all faith and hope.

Our hope lies in how these three continue to evolve and grow as God continues to expand our imaginations and capacities for them.

*****

For a minority today, only the material world is real. Their view of the existence of the universe is that through processes not yet understood, inanimate nonliving things gave rise to animated living things. Conscious, self-aware beings emerged out of objects that are neither conscious nor self-aware. That's the direction: from less complex to more complex.

Others of different religious perspective might narrate the rise of the universe differently. Animated consciousness precedes the inanimate matter that lacks consciousness. As the universe springs from a self-aware and conscious source then it makes sense that conscious and self-aware creatures rise from its waters. That's the direction: from consciously created matter to a self-aware creature.

This is how the ancients that wrote Genesis made sense of things. How many iterations it took to produce this result, we're not told. The Genesis story isn't an empirical account of the ultimate origins of all things but a story of beginnings, the story of the beginning of this thing we call consciousness.

By virtue of conscious self-awareness, we are connected to the mystery from which we emerge. While there may be a minority voice that claims an absolute knowledge that there is no God, faith in a creator is the majority view of humanity.

As strange as it may sound, regardless of how mysterious the universe is with black holes and dark energy, the greatest mystery in the universe may be us. We may solve the mysteries of the universe, but will we ever plumb the depths of what it means to be human?

We know that humankind is an animal that worships, a naturally religious animal. Religions reminds us that we battle the reality of evil— distortions of the human.

We know that the human is an animal that remembers and records, a historian. History reveals that we are masters of the inhumane—the less-than-human.

We know that the human is an animal that likes to understand, a scientist. Science, especially the field of genetics, points to our enhanced future — the trans-human.

But when it comes to knowing what it means to simply be human, we're amateurs.

We long to feel and sense the most beautiful things of the human experience. But we often feel powerless before the dehumanizing forces around us and within us.

That's our story.

We want to close the gap between what we are — our experiential state, our actuality — and what we imagine we can be — our dream state, our possibility.

No word captures the spirit of this better than the word hope.

Humanity is an aspiration we must pursue. It's a personal journey of discovered meaning, a cultural journey of transformation, and a species-wide evolution. And every person and culture within our species is at a slightly different place in the story.

At the species level, this journey has not been one of smooth incremental improvement. There's an analogy from evolutionary biology that seems to fit here. Evolutionary biologist Stephen Jay Gould who, when faced with a lack of evidence to support smooth evolutionary transitions between life forms, suggested a theory of revolutionary change called punctuated equilibrium.

Rather than taking the fossil evidence and forcing it to fit a gentle evolutionary curve, despite missing transitions that demonstrate a gradual passage of one species to another, he suggested that change must erupt suddenly (perhaps due to environmental changes) and created huge leaps in life forms. He felt this fit the fossil record better.

In the same way, becoming human has been a roundabout journey with setbacks and dead ends. We have also experienced seasons of "punctuated equilibrium" in which rapid change erupts to usher in new ages of enlightenment and new ways of becoming. This fits the historical record better.

For example, millions of years ago our ancient ancestors were little more than scavengers huddling together for warmth. Then someone from the tribe discovered how to make fire. This was our first and most important technological breakthrough moment. Suddenly everything profoundly and irrevocably changed for them and for us.

Hundreds of thousands of years later, an illiterate nomadic tribe receives ten words, a moral law, engraved in stone and Israel is born. That tribe was profoundly changed by this radical shift of perspective, and their social innovation changed the future for all humans.

Thousands of years later again, Jesus introduces a new understanding of compassion, community, value, and potential. The world is again profoundly changed through his death on a cross and the surprise of his resurrection. These aren't the only immense leaps towards becoming human, but they are major milestones of the journey, punctuation of the equilibrium.

What might the next major punctuation be?

It's a cosmic tragedy that our journey to become human is one of creating order out of disorder while the whole universe is on exactly the opposite journey. Physicists call it the second law of thermodynamics. The universe is dissolving, falling apart, moving towards chaos. It's a huge rotting tooth. The universe is not only indifferent to our yearnings for humanity, it works against it.

The journey to become human, to believe, hope, and love is an act of cosmic defiance.

We are a paradox. We are an anomaly of nature: evolutionary instinct coupled with revolutionary imagination covered in technological capacity to seed the universe with life. And all along we long for and pursue, each and every one of us, any and every clue to the meaning of us.

SHE
Flickers

The older men sat at the edge of camp, gesturing to the young men. Listening nearby, she absorbed every detail. From time to time when the men hit rocks together, and she would see flickers of light.

But the sparks always died and she knew why: fire doesn't eat rock. It needs dry grass and leaves, like the fires that lived seasonally on their savannah.

Early the next morning she gathered dry grass and leaves, the particular kinds of stones that threw sparks, and walked out of the village, not along the path toward water but toward the dark and stony hills nearby, where no path led.

She found the shadow of an overhang where she could work while the others rested during the heat of the day. She began to strike the stones together above a dried leaf. *If the flickers are indeed tiny fire, and they reach out to feed,* she thought, *perhaps they would live.*

She worked the combination of rocks that most often birthed the spark. The afternoon passed. Her knotted shoulders ached. But she persevered until, finally, a spark touched the dry tinder and a tiny hole opened. Her body froze.

She worked with greater determination now, for several days more, until suddenly another dry brown leaf started burning. Fingers trembling, she added more fuel, and tendrils of smoke curled around her bruised knuckles. As a gentle breeze blew, the heat burst into a small flame. She jerked away and stared with wide eyes.

She had given birth to fire. Soon the tiny fire died on its bed of gravel and she placed her hand above where it had momentarily blazed.

"…and the fire will test the quality of each person's work."

1 Corinthians 3.13

HEAT

Chapter 20

Sparks

I stood as quietly as possible on that dark night in the south african grass, heart pounding, hardly breathing. The swaying grass seemed to veil suspicious shadows.

Having deviated from the marked path, I now faced a decision. Should I continue forward through the grass and into the dark towards where I believed my cabin to be? Or, should I retrace my steps until I find the place where I lost the marked path?

I was startled by the sound of footsteps. My heart rate spiked. Then, one of the kitchen workers calmly sauntered by. As she approached I relaxed and pretended to be at ease. In as much of a "matter of fact" style as I could, I mentioned my cabin number to her with the inflection of a question.

She smiled and pointed in the direction of the dark.

I was hoping she would at least escort me to the lighted path if not all the way to my cabin. But instead she waved and walked her own way.

It was quiet again. And dark.

The third task of leadership is to discover new paths forward towards a more human world. But sometimes before we discover new paths, we need to discover the courage to walk the paths we already know. When we do, amazing things can happen.

*****

In our triangle of combustion, Fuel represents the "What" and Oxygen represents the "Why." Heat is the third ingredient needed to create a burning event. Heat represents the "How" of social transformation.

Heat is the ingredient of human choice. Neighborhoods, nations, and cultures change when a new Idea (or an old idea that has come of age) goes rogue. Often times the idea is attached to a person such as Ghandi, Darwin, Luther, Hitler, or Mandela.

In terms of leadership, the task of bringing the heat in the process of change can be broken down into three components.

First, in a time of exponential change, a leader must *describe and define* reality.

If I had to describe today's reality in one line, I would say that, within a culture that is tending towards disorder, we live at the beginning of a time of "redefinition."

To borrow an image from the Bible, our culture is "formless and void" but an "energy of creative order hovers over the face of the deep."

Fundamental structures of society such as marriage and family are being redefined. The nature of the Bible is being redefined. The role of church and government is being redefined. Even biological identifiers such as gender are being redefined.

These changes are happening so rapidly that leaders today must not only be aware of what's happening in the world, they must proactively be on the lookout for weak signals of even more oncoming change. This was the main idea behind section one: Fuel.

Second, because of the disorientation that people feel in times of exponential change, leaders must *discern* in the chaos meaning in life.

To make our time of redefinition even more complex, media keeps everyone alert to the fact that there are contrasting "redefinitions" emerging. Not everyone agrees on what marriage means, whether the United States is right or wrong, whether murdering infants in the womb is good or evil. Not everyone even agrees that there is such a thing as good and evil.

Leaders must look for meaning within the chaos. They must create compelling narratives, which give context and meaning to human existence, and in which others can cast themselves within a meaningful place to belong and a fair opportunity to become the people they desire.

For faith leaders this means learning to be comfortable in a setting in which their narrative is not the narrative of the majority, but of a niche. But "narrative" doesn't mean just a tagline. It means telling a story one deeply believes, and believing the story one tells enough to inhabit it.

This was the main idea behind section two: Oxygen.

Third, Leaders must nurture new communities which will create new ways forward. For church leaders and churches this will mean "living out" their story with daring and risk. Rather than seeing the Bible or tradition as a limiting factor, it needs to see these as launching pads for improvisation. There's an old joke that if, while playing a guitar, you hit a bad note, it's a mistake. If you hit two bad notes, again, it's a mistake. But of you hit three bad notes, it's jazz.

Well, no. It's not.

Improvisation is not just hitting any random note, as if anyone can do it. Improvisation is best accomplished by those who know the fret board best. When you know how a line is supposed to go and you deviate from it in search of something new and fresh, then you're improvising.

Leaders and communities who know their story well, believe it, and live it out, will need to improvise… will *want* to improvise …even if we hit a bad note here and again, in the pursuit of their mission.

To make gains in the public sphere, leaders will need to become media savvy because "social" is the new campfire around which the stories that shape us are being told. Story telling and story tellers will open up possibilities for the future. Communities that live out the future they prefer will redefine the world. Leading from certainty is over. Leading from possibility, from faith, hope, and love is the necessity.

*****

A nine-year-old Black boy was walking down the narrow sidewalk with his mother. At the same time, a tall white man in a dark suit was walking up the same sidewalk directly toward them.

The outcome of this scenario was predictable. The social etiquette of Johannesburg, South Africa, in the middle of the twentieth century, allowed for one set of predetermined behaviors. The young boy and his mother were to step off the sidewalk and let the white man pass; the man would do so without a glance or second thought. This was normal. This was expected. This was the social paradigm.

But every now and again in the human story, something unexpected happens and a paradigm shifts.

On that day, the tall man in the dark suit stepped off the sidewalk. As the young boy and his mother walked by him, the man tipped his hat to them in respect.

The boy asked his mother who that white man was.

"He is an Anglican priest," she told him.

There and then the young boy decided that when he grew up he would be one too. And that boy, named Desmond Tutu, did indeed grow up to be an Anglican priest– and, as a major voice in the South African struggle against apartheid, a powerful force for good in the world.

Makers of Fire are entrepreneurs of the spirit who spark change in their worlds. They, often against their wills, champion causes and create new communities around their values. They are also individuals who embody the change they want to see in the world.

To embody a change, to be the incarnation of a desired future, is an act of faith.

Often, like this Anglican priest, entrepreneurs of the spirit want to ignite the human imagination. They are dream whisperers who awaken hope. They connect meaning to action. They craft narratives that release human energy. They make new maps that guide us into places where there are no paths. As importantly, they help us discover the courage that it takes to journey towards our humanity.

Fire cannot happen without the heat of ignition. The Anglican priest chose an action that struck against the social norms, and sparks flew. I have known hundreds of women and men who dedicate themselves, like this priest, to igniting dreams within others. They are often alone in their cause at first. The human path can be lonely.

They act as they do because they see themselves engaged in an epic battle. It's a battle because the dangers on the "path of becoming human" are real and terrible. It's epic because the battle isn't restricted to Johannesburg in the 20th century. It extends to the very ends of the Earth today. And every person is engaged in this struggle to one degree or another.

If this Anglican priest was like the many heroes I have known, he not only wanted to do the right thing, he wanted to create a new universe of possibilities for the young boy and his mother.

He wanted to start a fire.

*****

Jesus was also a maker of fire, an entrepreneur of the spirit. His final speech ensured two ongoing realities. First, he ensured that those who followed him would be constant cross-cultural sparks of change. Second, he ensured that his followers would continue to grow and change themselves.

His last speech, as recorded in Matthew, was given after his resurrection. In it he instructed his disciples

" Therefore go and make disciples of all nations, baptizing them in the name of the Father and of the Son and of the Holy Spirit, and teaching them to obey everything I have commanded you. And surely I am with you always, to the very end of the age."

The practice of many today is to disciple the church, even though Jesus said, disciple all nations. Believers who have made the turn towards the nations, the outsider, are a link in the chain leading back to this saying of Jesus.

These fire making believers have shaped the future. As importantly, the faithful themselves have been changed in the process. Churches that haven't made this turn would experience less of the "other" and thus be less inclined to see their own blindnesses and biases and prejudices.

It's an irony of history that the same wave of exploration that brought merchants, traders, and others to exploit the world for Christian Europe also carried the fire making believers who came to include the nations in the life of Jesus.

But the fire makers went further. They took the message of Christ to places where merchants and nations would not prosper. And wherever new disciples of Jesus appeared, there followed communities of the spirit that were designed to cultivate the evolved capacities of faith, hope, and love.

These new communities were signposts of the future. They were sets of relationships that encouraged including the excluded and reaching out to the alien. These new communities were called the church.

*****

Another entrepreneur of the spirit who undoubtedly shared a profound affinity with the Anglican priest was a 1st century man known as the apostle Paul.

The New Testament was written in a world that operated on a slave economy. In his writings, Paul prescribed how one could best live for the glory of God within that system. He also personally undermined it. Like the Japanese sculptor, Etsuru Sotoo, who worked on the Sagrada Familia, a structure started by another artist, Antonio Gaudî, Paul asked the question, Where is the original designer taking this?

In his letter to Philemon, a first-century slave owner who was a convert to Christ, Paul makes an appeal for a runaway slave.

Why? Why would a freeman care for a slave?

To Paul, the slave isn't faceless. He has a name, Onesimus. And Paul appeals to Philemon based on their mutual allegiance to an invisible kingdom, the kingdom of Christ. The slave Onesimus has now become a believer and Paul refers to him in the letter as a "man," a "son," and a "brother." In other words, he isn't property. He's family. Paul cares for him because he now embraces him as part of the new community of the spirit of Christ.

This is fundamental to the biblical vision of a preferred future. All of us whether insider or outsider, slave or free are fellow humans, and all are part of the same family. This is the fundamental premise for the economy, politic, and religion of the future.

Within the slave economy, Onesimus was first and foremost Philemon's property, and Philemon could lawfully punish him severely. Paul writes to Philemon, *"...although in Christ I could be bold and order you to do what you ought to do, yet I prefer to appeal to you on the basis of love."* (Philemon 1.8-9)

There are two kingdoms in play here, and Paul and Philemon belong to them both. One is based on power. It's the sphere of the institution.

The other is based on love. It's the sphere of personal relationships that Christ creates on the human path.

Paul recognizes both spheres. He calls upon Philemon to focus on the familial relationships involved. He strikes the flint of a new way to understand "family" against the stony face of institutionalized social patterns.

He's hoping for sparks.

*****

We don't know what happened to Onesimus. It may have been too soon for him to benefit from the dream of a different world. But over time and for a variety of reasons slavery declined within Eurasia as the power of Rome declined and Christendom emerged. Then, with the discovery of the Americas, the slave trade surged again until only a couple of hundred years ago when Paul's incendiary ideas finally caught fire.

It's an anomaly that legalized slavery came to an end in the West. Slavery is more common in human history than liberty. Many of the West's leading enlightenment and humanist thinkers were pro-slavery. During the colonial period, many church leaders were pro-slavery. Somehow, in the end, individuals set ablaze with fiery passion organized gatherings often with the help of Christian congregations. The gatherings gained momentum and became movements that set political and economic worlds aflame.

In the UK it was a man named William Wilberforce who relentlessly pushed an abolitionist agenda, mobilized believers, and eventually triumphed. In the USA it was the Quakers who first became the Makers of Fire against the slaving industry. And to date, the West is the only culture throughout history in which there has been an indigenously-sparked movement of abolition.

Things just don't change. Makers of Fire change things.

Humans invented the expected set of behaviors in South Africa. But the Anglican priest rebelled against these patterns.

He had a different story he wanted to tell, a different story he wanted to inhabit. His story opened possibilities not available to others. In fact, his story contradicted the established story.

Meeting young Desmond presented for him a conscious clash of two cultures and their competing narratives—not European versus African culture, but South African Normal versus Jesus' Radically Human.

We are led astray by the assumption that our present moment is like every other moment. After all, "God is the same yesterday, today, and forever." And, "Human nature never changes."

But Makers of Fire recognize that today will indeed be just like yesterday, if we do nothing differently. This moment will indeed be just like the last, unless we embody the change we wish to see in the world.

What was going through Desmond Tutu's imagination after the incident? In his own recollections, Tutu tells us that his mind was filled with images of who and what he could become. The Anglican priest was, for young Desmond, a dream whisperer. His simple, gracious act burned in the young boy's heart a dream that would shape his future. It only took that moment for Tutu to catch a vision... for young Desmond to catch fire.

The Anglican bishop and young Desmond *discovered* a new way forward right on the spot. It was an act of improvisation by someone well rehearsed in the story of Christ. That is an ingredient of leading from the future.

Creating the future does not begin with a plan. It begins with a dream. And when someone acts on the dream, it creates a spark.

Chapter 21

Incoming Firestorms

When thinking about igniting change we have to ask, What do we mean by change? By change I mean: to make the future course of human relationships different from what they have been, are, or would be if left alone.

The forces of change travels in two directions. First, there is inbound change. These are the things that come at us from the outside. Second, there is outbound change. These are the things, decisions, actions that happen within our organization or within us personally and that we send out towards others.

Why change comes when it does is a mystery. A part of it has to do with communications that allow rogue ideas to spread. The Romans built roads that created better travel and communication throughout the empire. The events of Jesus' life spread like wild fire along these travel routes. Johannes Gutenberg invented the Printing Press in 1454. Without it Martin Luther's thesis, that led to a revolution that spanned the entirety of western culture, may have remained a very local issue. Today we have social media that allows news to travel around the world in seconds.

Whatever the reasons change comes when it does, there seem to be at least three Events that ignite change: Contact with Outsiders, Significant Events, and Epiphanies.

*****

Historically, change often comes to a society through contact with another society. For example, much of the world today can only be understood through the expansion of the British Empire. During their tenure as rulers of the world, the

English invaded all but 22 countries. British culture has left its fingerprints all over the world.

Even a country as populous as India was radically shaped by British presence. The Indian practice and institution of "widow burning" in which a man's wife would be burned with him when he dies, was made illegal by the British in the 19th century. English is now another of India's many languages. India's form of government is based on the English parliamentary system. British culture was an inbound or incoming force driving change.

Transformation through contact with others is an essential underpinning of the Christian faith. When Christ gave his final instructions to his disciples, he commissioned them to disciple the nations. But rather than making contact as an act of war or exploitation, Jesus' disciples were to make contact as an act of love.

In doing so, he assured not only that his disciples would constantly stir change in the world. He insured that his own movement and his own future disciples would, through this contact with other peoples, be constantly changing themselves. Contact with others motivated by love is a part of the transformational process of discipleship. It is an important part of how we become human.

There is an insight here about social change that must be highlighted. Jesus, history's maven of human transformation, placed more weight on his disciples than he did on governments as a force for positive change in the world.

*****

A second way change happens is through significant events. The events of September 11, 2001 were an inbound driver of change. But not all change is initiated from the outside.

In April of 1992, I walked through the fires and rubble of South Central Los Angeles. As part of my work I had been conducting some social research in this part of the city. Even though we were warned not to enter the area, I felt a responsibility to check in on some of the residents with whom I had made contact.

The scene reminded me of a war zone. I watched as people ran down the streets with electronics and other goods looted from neighborhood shops to the backdrop of burning buildings. The odd thing was that these people were acting like they had just won a lottery. They were not the stereotypical south-central gang bangers. They looked like mothers and sisters and students. It was as if the spirit of chaos had swept through and dispossessed an entire community of its senses.

The igniting event was the beating of an African American named Rodney King. The technology that captured the event was a clunky Sony Handycam in the hands of local resident George Holliday, who heard sirens just outside his Lake View Terrace apartments, stepped out on his balcony, and filmed the whole episode. This is an example of change within culture that is both inbound and outbound depending on your point of view. This significant event came at us all through media even though it happened right around us.

The beating of Rodney King had meaning far beyond the singular event. It manifested two aspects of change sweeping the world. First, the use of technology foreshadowed how technology would and could be used to gain a global hearing. The second was an expression of a significant global shift in attitude with regard to the relationship of power to the oppressed.

Technologically, every police officer now operates in a YouTube culture. The world has their eyes on those who exercise power. In April of 1992 not everyone had a camcorder and fewer carried one with them daily. In today's mobile-phone culture, everyone's a filmmaker. The Rodney King video relied on television stations to spread it through the culture and repeat it often enough to engrave it on people's minds, which took days and weeks. If the Rodney King incident were to happen today, it would be online and viral within minutes.

Technology makes it far more difficult for "empires" to hide behind the curtain of secrecy. They must act in public. Freedom of internet access is a human right when viewed in relationship to power. We should make sure that access to this technology of liberty spreads to every person on Earth, especially the billion least likely to be connected. Technology could form a protective sphere against the powers of empire —whether that empire is a nationstate, a corporation, or a local bully.

The second shift is attitudinal. The 1990s were marked by a significant demonstration of this sweeping change of mind that seized the planet. The demise of the Soviet union, the tearing down of the Berlin wall (1989), the anonymous "tank man" who brought a column of Type 59 tanks to a halt, were all signs, but not of the triumph of capitalism over communism. They were signs of a shift away from centralized power and towards an idyllic "flatter and more democratic world."

Today's mobile technology coupled with an attitudinal change that favors the underdog, the minority, and challenges centralized power, points toward new social sensitivities being born. We all are more suspicious of centralized power.

This is trending in the direction of the Genesis 1 human society. It is the democratization of the image of God. But this democratization is still not fully realized among us. There is still a long way to go before this portion of scripture is "true."

The Genesis 1 image of human society is a prophetic projection of an idealized human future, not a picture of a time lost in the past. The function of this image is for us to "make it so," for us to create this future.

There was a time when Rodney King's beating would not have raised any social uproar. That time is gone. But we shouldn't take it for granted.

Today, we can post a video to YouTube and expect an uprising. This hasn't always been the case, and this may not always be the case. We are more sensitive to the plight of the oppressed and of the individual than perhaps ever before in human history. We have mindscapes forged in the furnace of an ongoing rebellion against centralized power.

That may be why so many of those who strongly oppose gay marriage still love the idea of protecting gay civil rights and of going the extra mile to make sure this tiny minority is protected.

But the inbound change cause by contact with outsiders and by significant events aren't the only drivers of change. There are also epiphanies.

*****

An epiphany is an experience of sudden insight or of a striking realization. In the scriptures epiphanies happen in conjunction with theophanies, sudden manifestations of God. We could argue that epiphanies create outbound change because they happen within us. But theophanies, assuming the activity of an external and personal God, is an inbound source of personal and social change.

The Hebrew scriptures tell us that change came to Israel when it encountered God in the wilderness. For years they had suffered as slaves in Egypt. After a four hundred year silence, God introduced himself to Moses, who was herding sheep, and spoke to him through a "burning bush."

God sent Moses to Egypt to lead his people to a land he had promised their ancestor named Abraham. As they traveled between their history as slaves in Egypt and their futurity as a people with their own land, they struggled with their own sense of identity. They doubted Moses. They doubted God. They doubted themselves. For forty years they wandered in the wilderness while they tried to figure out where their story was going.

It was there in the desert that something remarkable happened. According to the story, God personally writes something down. God wrote ten words for Moses as a moral code for his people. Theophany becomes epiphany: God cares about how we treat one another.

Contact with outsiders, significant events, and epiphanies/ theophanies are the kinds of experiences that drive change. Change today is an ongoing constant because our web based connectedness puts us in constant contact with outsiders, makes us aware of the significant events happening everywhere, and offers us a view into the world we live in, our beautiful and broken world.

Chapter 22

THE FIRE MAKERS

Besides Contact with outsiders, significant events, and epiphanies, human creativity also brings the heat of ignition. "Creation," said billionaire John Hammond in the popular movie, Jurassic Park, "is an act of the will." Entrepreneurs of the spirit are willful. They do what they do, not because some laws says they must, but because they have been transformed by a vision of a preferred future.

I work with a network of leaders through the International Mentoring Network (IMN). In 2004 the IMN launched an action research project called Voxtropolis. The general idea was to launch and nurture communities of creativity. These communities shared the goal of inspiring their neighborhoods to be less consumeristic and more creative. At the same time these communities wanted to raise awareness for local and global needs.

While birthed out of a desire to live out a Jesus inspired life, the Voxtropolis platform was not a religious platform. It was based on a belief in "common grace" and on platform for the "common good." The project focused on creating a conversation around a singular question: What does it mean to be human? We called the events themselves, Culture Pubs or Creativity Lounges.

Educator and entrepreneur of the spirit Eric Sweiven was one of the first to jump in. He wanted local artists in Sacramento get more exposure for their art. At the same time he wanted to make a difference in the community.

He launched Vox in Sacramento where he hosted art exhibitions to raise awareness for a variety of social issues from sex trafficking to domestic abuse and violence. With little to no budget, but plenty of passion, Eric tapped into a need that was waiting just below the surface. Leading from the future includes the ability to discover new ways forward.

Social and spiritual entrepreneur, Ted Law, soon followed with Vox Culture in Houston. Like Vox in Sacramento, they inspire communal creativity, speak out on important social issues like domestic violence, and are advocates for great local charities.

Music producer and entrepreneur of the spirit, Chris Miles, followed suite in Montreal. Chris builds community through events he hosts in a local bar. One of his events, for example, was designed to help a homeless shelter that uses art therapy. Besides performances by local musicians, homeless artists had an opportunity to exhibit and sell their art.

Entrepreneur of the spirit, cartoonist, and dream whisperer Geoffrey Baines sat with me at the first ever meeting of Voxtropolis in Montreal. He was so inspired by what Chris and his team were doing that he decided to make fire in his town of Edinburgh. He scouted about town, discovered artistic talent he wanted to promote, and found a receptive cafe in the Fountainbridge area of the city. He designed a first event to raise money to buy mosquito nets in Africa.

More recently Geoffrey's creativity movement has, in his words: "...needed a black box space to explore collaborations chosen by the community: music and dance, text and textile, and, 3D projection and 2D art. Whilst our artists and artisans are mostly in their 20s and 30s, we gather people of all ages, and we are seeking to write a story together about how our art-works can make a difference in the lives of others."

Their collaborative efforts raise money to invest in entrepreneurs in the developing world.

Our action research across a dozen cities focused on learning how to create communities of creatives that work together towards the common good outside of a religious platform. It's also been a process to help young spiritual entrepreneurs and established leaders gain a field-based experience with the art of ignition.

*****

Executive coach and award winning entrepreneur Hermann Du Plessis launched the International Mentoring Network - South Africa (IMNSA) in 2009 with mentoring discussions at Monash University in Johannesburg. He and his wife Adel, a social entrepreneur, business manager, and lecturer in financial accounting, gathered a team of engineers, bankers, pastors, lawyers, accountants, and the unemployed, to serve as mentors for aspiring entrepreneurs from all races and economic classes.

They are entrepreneurs of the spirit who want to help spread the art of making fire.

Adel uses her expertise to train women of color to succeed in South Africa's business culture. At the same time she helps corporations recognize the cultural and economic benefits of hiring women of color.

Hermann and Adel's team also trains entrepreneurs. Recently the IMNSA guided a young man named Peter, for example, who grew up in Kwa-Zulu Natal, but came to Johannesburg for better opportunities in 2007. Peter did piecemeal jobs, on a day to day basis, for less than minimum wage. With the help of the IMNSA's mentoring and training Peter eventually landed a post as a regional manager for an international corporation.

But the IMNSA also ignited Peter's entrepreneurial spirit. Beyond succeeding at his new job, he also launched his own recycling business to serve his community. From living in a humble shack alone to being married and living in a middle class suburb, from riding public transport to owning his own car, Peter's future is different because of the IMN's makers of fire.

And now Peter himself is a fire-making entrepreneur of the spirit.

This is change at its most elemental stage, the personal.

Makers of Fire alter the course of events and relationships from what they were, are, or would have been, if left alone.

*****

Some think social change is always born at the institutional level of power. When we get a law, that's when social change happens. But a law or a policy is only an aspect of social change. It is the punctuation of the dynamics of change that are happening before and continue to happen after laws are passed.

For a current example, consider the evolution of President Obama's public position of same-sex marriage. While campaigning for President, Barack Obama did not support same sex marriage. He evolved on the issue while in office and by 2012 he did support same-sex marriage. Today he believes, according to The New Yorker, that the Constitution requires all States to allow same -sex marriage. That's a radical about face.

Here's the revealing comment from the article. The actions of the Supreme Court, that decided to not rule on same-sex marriage but allow the process to play out in the States, sent to Obama "…a powerful signal of the changes that have taken place in society and that the law is having to catch up."

Exactly.

Change often comes *to* the top, not *from* it.

Change can come from the top down. This kind of change begins with the imposition of new behaviors and practices. This leads to conformity that may over time shapes mindsets.

But the law often waits for change before embracing it. So do politicians. Consider how change came in the USA when it comes to same sex marriage, recreational marijuana, and singleness.

It begins with pop culture media. Media is the modern equivalent of the Roman Empire's roads that facilitated commerce, communication, and the spread of ideas. It performs the same functions (and more) as the printing press that accelerated the spread of ideas even more during Luther's day.

Popular television shows placed these social issues in a favorable light, with humor. Whether it be shows like Will and Grace, Modern Family, Weeds, or, reaching back a little bit, Murphy Brown, pop culture shapes us all.

The social reality of these ideas is sustained by communities or networks of "elites," the "avante garde," or the cultural creatives, who adopt or express support for these changes.

Eventually the adoption of these ideas includes localized social acceptance such as Massachusetts embracing same sex marriage or Colorado's permitting recreational Marijuana use.

After pop culture media, the 21st century tribal fire of story telling, tells the story and begins to redefine the cultural narrative, and celebrities begin to advocate these changes, and local support begins to grow, and money begins to flow, then politicians and laws will follow.

These social changes came from the grass roots, driven by media, to the top. The top — the courts and politicians and C-Suites of major corporations — will embrace the change through law, policy, and practice. Then it will enforce the law and impose change on those who lag behind until the society is conformed.

But there is a difference between conformity and transformation. Why would Eric, Ted, Chris, Geoffrey, Johnny, Hermann, Adel, and others make such an effort? Because there is a burning in their hearts to make the world human. This burning calls these kinds of entrepreneurs of the spirit to strike a rock, make a spark, work towards ignition, and make fire.

There is no law for that.

*****

Johnny K'Nell saw a sign that captured his attention. He instinctively did something out of the ordinary. He made a u-turn and discovered a house that served children who had suffered massive burns. An experience designer, brand marketer, and spiritual entrepreneur, Johnny created a series of experiences which gathered local artists in his city of Johannesburg and put together a benefit called Beauty from the Ashes in support of the house. And this was just the beginning of ongoing efforts to help create a new future for Johannesburg and its residents.

Some people dream of making a difference. Others turn their cars around. The future doesn't begin with a plan. It begins with a dream. But if we don't act on the dream, fire will never happen.

Makers of Fire are those who act on their dreams. They are entrepreneurs of social and spiritual change. By *change* I mean "to make the future course of human relationships different than they were, are, or would be if left alone." By *entrepreneur* I mean "someone who organizes, manages, and assumes the risks of a new insight, movement, business or enterprise."

The word entrepreneur comes from an Old French word meaning "to undertake." An entrepreneur is one who takes "initiative, trying to create something new cognizant of the risks involved." I use the term here in an expanded sense, one that includes business but also transcends it.

Entrepreneur and financial consultant Dave Ramsey writes, "Entrepreneurs, as a whole, are natural risk-takers. They are confident and know what it takes to get the job done. Nothing gets in their way."

On the other hand, William Sahlman of the Harvard Business School says that entrepreneurs are *not* risk seekers. They are *reward* seekers and are more than happy to let others take the risk.

Two smart guys. Opposite ideas. They both look at entrepreneurs through the filter of business. We include these kinds of entrepreneurs under the rubric of Makers of Fire. We also go further.

Today there is a lot of excitement around the idea of the social entrepreneur. A social entrepreneur is an entrepreneur who has an added bottom line, that of social benefit. These are entrepreneurs who undertake a cause and assume the risk. They want to make an impact in the world, not just on their wallet. They ask questions like, How can I make a profit and a positive impact in my community?

*****

These entrepreneurs find their counterpart in an ancient man not known for his entrepreneurship but for his apostleship. His name was Peter.

Although we don't have evidence of it, Peter most likely grew up working in the fishing industry. We do know that when he met Jesus, he was a fisherman. He belonged to a Jewish family and as such learned to maintain a religiously crucial distance between himself and those who were not Jews, the gentiles. He would never eat with gentiles. That would be taboo. And because as a people the Jews had their own diet he would never eat a gentile's foods.

After Jesus' resurrection, Peter became a leader in the Christ-following movement. Once while he was praying in the middle of the day, he had a vision. The vision consisted of unclean foods lowered from heaven for Peter to eat. Peter, of course, could not eat such food. But a voice said to him, "Do not call unclean what God has cleaned." The meaning of the vision became clear when Peter received a visit from representatives of a gentile man named Cornelius. They claimed that God had sent an angel to Cornelius instructing him to send for Peter.

Peter would never enter a gentile's home. But the resurrection of Christ, destabilized his worldview. The resurrection led to a time of dismantling and redefinition, not unlike our own. In this new world, the unthinkable became doable.

Peter acted upon his vision in ways impossible to him before. He traveled to Cornelius' house and as he crossed the threshold of this gentile home, he broke a religious and cultural taboo.

This is where Peter's problems began and where his work as an entrepreneur of social change shines. The result of this seemingly small encounter had huge implications. Soon other believers, who like Peter were Jewish, began to question Peter' wisdom. (Sometimes even the smallest act of humanity may cause immense reactions in a social system.)

How Peter responds as an entrepreneur of social change is instructive for us even today. The story is told in the New Testament book of Acts, chapters ten and eleven.

"The apostles and believers throughout Judea heard that the gentiles also had received the word of God. So when Peter went up to Jerusalem, the

circumcised believers criticized him and said, 'You went into the house of uncircumcised men and ate with them.'" (Acts 11. 1-3)

This critique reflected an immutable social norm. Jews don't enter the houses of uncircumcised men (gentiles), much less eat with them. This norm was part of their social foundation.

There are lots of ways Peter could have reacted to this criticism. But the account tells us: *"Starting from the beginning, Peter told them the whole story."* Rather than reacting defensively, or arrogantly rolling his eyes because these fellows "just don't get it," he allows them the opportunity to see through his eyes.

Here we see four practices of social entrepreneurs of change.

1) They are people who dream. Peter prayed, meditated, and once was even seized by visions. These entrepreneurs experience a change within themselves that demands to be worked out through their lives.

2) They act on their vision and embody it in tangible ways. This gives them stories to tell.

3) They tell the stories their dreams and visions have woven into their lives.

4) They persuade and influence others.

Science has a method for evaluating evidence. Mathematics has proofs. Logic has inferences and syllogisms. Faith has stories. If words are sounds with purpose, stories are words grouped together and spoken with intention.

Peter rehearses his experience in detail to his listeners. He tells them that, like them, he resisted the idea of violating their ancient taboo. He explained the coincidence that just as his vision ended, the representatives of Cornelius knocked on the door. He added that the Spirit told him not to hesitate but to go with them. While speaking to Cornelius in his home, Peter tells them, the Spirit came upon Cornelius' household, even as the Spirit had come upon Peter and his Jewish brothers and sisters earlier. Peter concludes, "*if God gave them the same gift as he gave us who believed in the Lord Jesus Christ, who was I to think that I could stand in God's way?*" (Acts 11.17)

Peter lays out before them the events that led to his own transformation. He identified with his audience. He proclaims his truth through a narrative. The narrative exerts its natural power of inviting the listener to enter the experience.

Politicians use propaganda and legislation to achieve conformity to their social agendas. Social entrepreneurs of change use the power of story, affinity (the identification of common ground), and personal invitation to change what we care about.

"*When they heard this,*" the story in Acts tells us, "*they had no further objections and praised God, saying, 'So then, even to Gentiles God has granted repentance that leads to life.*" They began to understand that the resurrection of Christ was not just a matter of belief, it had implications for social structure.

*****

This is a useful process for entrepreneurs of change. Returning to the combustion triangle, **a social movement lives on the Oxygen of meaning.** Spiritual and Social entrepreneurs often have something other entrepreneurs don't. That is a sense of calling. They are not just driven by ambition — something I consider good. They are invited by a calling. Something I consider amazing.

In your case, your task may be to cultivate an urban garden to provide fresh produce for an under served area, or to teach a tribe the art of aquaponics so they can farm their own fish and water based vegetables, or to help marginalized people find access to training and education, or to employ the homeless to make sleeping bags for homeless populations. In Peter's case, the task was to communicate the gospel, the story about resurrection of Jesus Christ and what it meant for the listeners, the tellers, and the world.

Wherever your own purpose calls you, understanding Peter's process for change will help you ignite social transformations.

*****

While some entrepreneurs are about business and profit — and that's a good thing — other entrepreneurs are about business, profit, and benefit to the community.

Examples of Fire Making Entrepreneurs include:

1) For-Profits. Entrepreneurs who start for-profit businesses that have a profoundly embedded social conscience in their DNA. Their concern isn't just the "bottom line" but also the net benefit they bring to their community.

House Blend Cafe in central Florida, whose tagline is "Eat Good Do Good" is an example. Their website states their vision: "The concept of HOUSE BLEND CAFE developed over the course of several years of dreaming of a creative way to connect with people, impact lives and see community happen the way it's supposed to."

The locally owned business offers tons of support to its community and to the world. Their contributions include partnering with local social services, offering mentoring to area kids, cultivating an organic farm, bringing aquaponics to the nations, and returning 100% of their net profit to the community.

2) Social Non-profits. Entrepreneurs who start nonprofit social projects.

Life Remodeled, launched and led by entrepreneur of the spirit, Chris Lambert, in Detroit is an example. Life Remodeled is a non-profit organization that exists to remodel lives—one neighborhood at a time. From their web site: "Our strategy includes remodeling a Detroit Public School each summer in order to create academic and athletic improvements. Additionally, we believe that if we partner with the local residents to remove blight in the surrounding area and create safe and inspirational pathways to the school, we will help to sustain and build up a neighborhood that radiates hope to the rest of the city!"

3) Prophetic Non-profits. Then you have prophetic entrepreneurs, those solitary individuals who carry the financial and emotional burden for a cause, often alone for years, until it's taken up by others. I don't use the term "prophetic" here to suggest anything like "predicting the future." The future can't be predicted. I use it here in the sense that a prophet, like the Old testament prophets, keeps making visible what the rest of society wishes was invisible.

Elevate Detroit is an example. What started with a couple of concerned citizens hosting a cookout with the poor and homeless, even in the cold Michigan winters, became a place where all kinds of people would gather regardless of their housing conditions. This is a kind of prophetic ministry that serves to remind the rest of us the about the things that matter to God. Mike Schmitt, the driving force behind Elevate Detroit, fires up his barbecue every Saturday, even in the freezing snow.

Mike and his Barbecue are a sign of a possible future, when no one is left outside and everyone is welcome at the table. The prophetic entrepreneur of social change is the category of every person who takes an opportunity to make a difference in the world at their own expense. Elevate Detroit has grown to be far more than just a solitary figure crying in the wilderness. Others have seen the unseen vision that Mike carries and have joined along.

4) Multi-dimensional, Communal Entrepreneurs of the Spirit

In recent years the difficult economic conditions of the city of Detroit has received a lot of attention. Several of the examples used in this list are from the Detroit area. Another kind of entrepreneurship is embodied in a community called Micah 6.

The Micah 6 community may be one of the most exciting things happening in southeast Michigan. Coleman Yoakum's team and their work in Pontiac Michigan falls into several categories. The city of Pontiac, one of the many devastated zones in Southeast Michigan, is characterized by a highly transient population. This made a sense of community scarce within the city.

Rather than serve the city from the outside, Coleman decided to move into the city with a half a dozen friends and create what it really needed: neighbors.

They bought a house and began to buy empty lots where he planted orchards and community gardens. They then leased a corner property to make fresh produce, which is nowhere accessible nearby, available to the community.

Their work takes the name Micah 6 community taken from the Old Testament book named Micah with a focus on chapter 6 and verse 8: "*He has made it clear to you, mortal man, what is good and what the LORD is requiring from you— to act with justice, to love mercy, and to walk humbly with your God.*" (Micah 6.8)

Coleman and his team are unusual examples of embodiment. He is an entrepreneur of social and spiritual change who dares to incarnate the future he seeks to create. And he calls others to embody this future with him.

Social, prophetic, and spiritual entrepreneurs are included among those I've been calling "Makers of Fire." They intuitively exhibit the three traits common to future-oriented leaders.

First, they are profoundly "in touch" with what is happening around them. Because they are tuned into the present, they are able to *describe* and *define* the reality of the present moment for others.

Second, they have a vision, a strong sense of their preferred future. In other words, they *discern* the meaning and need of the moment.

Third, they step into the fray and strategically set out to create the future they envision and call on others to join them. In other words, they *discover* creative paths forward towards a more human world.

Fire happens when we add the heat of ignition to fuel and oxygen. Social change becomes possible when human choices activate the human need for meaning in culturally sensitive ways. The leadership task is *describing* the present, *discerning* the meaning, and *discovering* creative paths towards a world that works for everyone.

When that happens a burning event become possible.

*****

The social disruptions experienced by the decline of the traditional (European) churches in the USA is not the whole story of faith in the west. While the Christ-following movement has institutional and denominational expressions, it is primarily a community of the spirit.

Christ following communities form under the umbrella of these institutions, but they form outside the authority and reach of the institution as well. In fact, as a grassroots movement, the communities of the spirit are always changing, adapting, evolving, and restarting.

Within their industry, those who start new churches to serve new populations are called "church planters." Thousands of new churches are started in the USA each year, and tens of thousands around the world. For those of you not familiar with this phenomenon, a new church does not mean a new church building. It means a new gathering that may inhabit a house, school, cafe, a park, or anywhere that new community of faith finds suitable.

Some closely follow the pattern of their brand, franchise, or "denomination," others explore creative ways to organize new local manifestations of faith. The Green Room in Ann Arbor is an example. This new church started by actors and entrepreneurs of the spirit, Scott and Denise Crownover, for others in the theatre industry is one of the most creative new churches in the country. They currently meet on Monday night which is the "dark night" that is, the night when the theatre is closed, and place a heavy emphasis on creativity and compassion.

Another such spiritual entrepreneur is Diallo Smith who, along with his wife, Jameel, have launched both Awakenings Movement Church and The Drive Table Tennis Social Club to serve the city of Detroit. Drive is a for profit business and Awakenings is designed to give residents of Detroit an alternative to the traditional faith communities that abound in the Motor City.

Whether it's Lorenzo Della Foresta, who started a new church in Montreal when others told him it couldn't be done, Mark Juane, starting a new church in Toronto, or Sam and Rachel Radford in Sheffield (UK), new churches are signals of possible futures.

The church was designed to be an alternative future in our midst. Has this always been the case? No. But the resources for such communities are embedded within the stories and traditions of the faith. Starting new churches is a strategy to create the future.

This is a strange fact when we consider that the church around the world pays a lot of attention to the past. Every Sunday we rehearse the things God did...in Israel, in the early church, in Jesus...in the past.

In church, we remember.

The book the church reads is an ancient one. True, many churches seek to apply ancient wisdom to the present moment, but the emphasis is always on bringing forward the past.

Because the Christ following faith is based on it's history, we would never want to lose this emphasis. We must remember.

And, because the faith announces a risen Christ who is with us on the great adventure to disciple the nations, we also want to keep the emphasis on our present experience. We must experience the reality of the Kingdom now. We are a people of the spirit.

But what of the future? Do we have a vision of a preferred future that we'd like to bring into the right here and right now?

The disciple-making process called "church planting" is one way the church intentionally faces outward and forward. Church planting anticipates and creates new communities of faith. In other words, church planters work to create future communities of faith with future new disciples of Jesus.

Because the audience for a new church is that population of people who do not yet follow Christ, there is an incredible opportunity to create future communities of faith that reflect a vision of the future rather than the restrictions of the past.

To launch a new community of faith means that believers can learn from the past and unlearn the bad stuff. They can create new future communities of faith that more clearly reflect the world changing stories believers rehearse. Because old churches can become rigid as they rehearse the old in their particular way, it is often far more difficult for them to enter into the future. Too often they are concerned with saving the past.

But with new churches, this is not a concern. With new churches, believers can create the future.

But according to what belief do we imagine the future we are to create? Where is the human story going?

The biblical story is a spiritual resource that offers many trajectories for the creation of the human future. I find three of these trajectories fundamental.

First, the remarkable idea that all human kind is made in the image of God. This idea seems so out of place in the ancient world. In fact, it's out of place in much of the world today. So many humans are dismissed as lower quality life forms.

This trajectory was forged in a world in which the Emperor was the image of God, but it suggests a future in which every human being is cherished as invaluable. This is a fragile idea, a trajectory that is vulnerable to our worst instincts. It shouldn't be taken for granted.

Second, the incredible idea that the female and the male are both equally created in the image of God. A quick survey of history and even of the world today leads me to ask, Where in the world could this idea have come from? It's easier to believe that this idea was brought to earth by some extra-terrestrial intelligence than it is an idea originated by humans. But there it is, embedded within the scriptures. This is another fragile trajectory that has much, much farther to go.

Third, the idea described earlier that everyone is "us." In a world of tribal war and hatred, God called Abraham to "friend" all the families on Earth.

Sometimes people ask me if I believe the Bible is true. When I think of these trajectories I think the Bible is not true (yet), but it ought to be. And I think that is the genius of this spiritual resource. It is a call for us to join God in creating a human future together.

I suggest that Jesus is a signal from the future. He is where the human story is going. When the story of Christ is told, these three trajectories are advanced.

The best way believers can create a human future is to care about the things Jesus cared about, to love the ways he loved, to lead the way he led.

Remember the ancient stories.

Experience the reality of the spirit now.

Create the future.

Leading from the future must engage the past and the future to create the present we desire.

Another way to look at the Triads of Fire which leaders and communities of the spirit inhabit is as a GPS for navigating the white water culture of complexity and exponentially rapid change. This final triad is:

(1) Knowledge. They are aware of the fuel of the culture around them. They keep up with the "what?" And they fearlessly describe what they see.

(2) Intuition. They know communities need the oxygen of meaning. They seek to understand the "why?" And they thoughtfully discern the meaning in the mix.

(3) Courage. They know that creativity is needed to advance the human story. They have the courage to walk where there is no path and discover ways forward.

These also correspond to the Triangle of Combustion.

(1) Fuel =   Knowledge | Experience

(2) Oxygen=   Intuition | Wisdom

(3) Heat=   Courage | Love

Chapter 23

Burn

In the days following the gruesome death of Jesus of Nazareth, two men were walking from Jerusalem towards a small town called Emmaus. On their way they were joined by a third man. They did not recognize that the man was Jesus. How could they? Their experience of life, like ours, told them that the dead don't return. And we cannot see what we cannot believe.

Most people today are religious or spiritual in some way, but there are those who dismiss the possibility of events they cannot explain. Even though practically everything we do today would seem like unexplainable magic to those who lived one hundred years ago, some skeptics avoid any line of thinking that might seem to have a supernatural patina.

If resurrection from the dead is impossible and must be logically excluded as an option, then the mysterious events around Jesus' death must have another explanation. Because *we all know*, as did those two men on their way to Emmaus, that the dead cannot return.

*****

This story, told only by Luke, describes how Makers of Fire creatively engage existing artifacts, the Fuel of the world, to describe a new vision of reality, the Oxygen of life, and with those things, ignite a fire in the hearth of the human heart.

Now that same day two of them were going to a village called Emmaus, about seven miles from Jerusalem. They were talking with each other about everything that had happened. As they talked and discussed these things with each other, Jesus himself came up and walked along with them; but they were kept from recognizing him.

He asked them, "What are you discussing together as you walk along?"

They stood still, their faces downcast. One of them, named Cleopas, asked him, "Are you the only one visiting Jerusalem who does not know the things that have happened there in these days?"

"What things?" he asked.

"About Jesus of Nazareth," they replied. "He was a prophet, powerful in word and deed before God and all the people. The chief priests and our rulers handed him over to be sentenced to death, and they crucified him; but we had hoped that he was the one who was going to redeem Israel. And what is more, it is the third day since all this took place. In addition, some of our women amazed us. They went to the tomb early this morning but didn't find his body. They came and told us that they had seen a vision of angels, who said he was alive. Then some of our companions went to the tomb and found it just as the women had said, but they did not see Jesus."

He said to them, "How foolish you are, and how slow to believe all that the prophets have spoken! Did not the Messiah have to suffer these things and then enter his glory?" And beginning with Moses and all the Prophets, he explained to them what was said in all the Scriptures concerning himself.

As they approached the village to which they were going, Jesus continued on as if he were going farther. But they urged him strongly, "Stay with us, for it is nearly evening; the day is almost over." So he went in to stay with them.

When he was at the table with them, he took bread, gave thanks, broke it, and began to give it to them. Then their eyes were opened and they recognized him, and he disappeared from their sight. They asked each other, "Were not our *hearts burning within us while he talked with us on the road and opened the Scriptures to us?"*

They got up and returned at once to Jerusalem. There they found the Eleven and those with them, assembled together and saying, "It is true! The Lord has risen and has appeared to Simon." Then the two told what had happened on the way, and how Jesus was recognized by them when he broke the bread. (Luke 24.13-35)

When the Fuel of culture — in this story, the events in Jerusalem concerning the life of Jesus — met the Oxygenating flow of meaning — in this story, the disoriented pilgrims who were struggling with their understanding of the world and their scriptures — and were ignited by the Heat of human creativity — in this story, Jesus' new interpretation of the Hebrew scriptures — there results a burn, a release of energy.

Here's the heart of the beautiful text:

*"They asked each other, "**Were not our hearts burning within us** while he talked with us on the road and opened the Scriptures to us?"*

The two men experience their hearts "burning" within them. By "heart" I mean that place in the brain where the emotions meet reason, mobilize the will, and shape identity.

Transformation cannot be imposed by force. It can't be mandated by government and law. It comes with the acceptance of new meaning.

Makers of Fire make the human heart burn.

The events of their hike to Emmaus, more than two thousand years ago, marked a localized and contextualized heart-shift that proved to be globally scalable and cross-culturally contagious. It spread virally from person to person.

Every believer in the world today can be traced back through relationships, like links in an unbroken chain, all the way back to those who knew Jesus.

That's what happened with young Desmond and the Anglican priest. The burn that began in and around the resurrection of Christ eventually reached the Anglican's heart, and then Desmond Tutu's heart, and continues to burn in hearts today. The heart is the hearth where the fuel of culture and the oxygen of purpose wait for the incendiary spark of creativity.

The heart is *where* change begins.

Relationships are *how* the change begins.

Fire is an exothermic chemical reaction. It's a process by which the fuel that is consumed breaks down and new molecular compounds form. That which burns is fundamentally transformed.

When the fires of change come, the world is made new again. Some may never be able to believe in this new world until they see it.

Makers of fire know that you will never see this new world until you first believe in it.

Chapter 24

Abraham in Space

Abraham's choice to migrate, the creativity of his imagination, and his leadership genius ignited the fuel of his world with new meaning.

Abraham was not a theologian in any professional sense. He was a clever negotiator and business person. He was an urbanite chieftain who left the city towards an uncertain but promising future. In many ways, he was like you. A person trying to make his mark in the world.

To say Abraham broke with the wheel, the cyclical view of time, does not mean that he became a secular 21st century thinker. While Abraham broke from the wheel, he did not separate the spiritual from the physical. While, for Abraham, time did take on a more linear dimension, it was still tied to eternity. But rather than spirit manifesting itself in the recurring cycles of nature, spirit manifested itself in a developing drama within history.

Abraham creates the future, but he sees it as the path upon which eternity breaks in. For him eternity can take the shape of time and time the contours of eternity. For him the dream and the deed coincide.

And, while Abraham set the stage for the rise of western culture, and maybe even the modern myth of progress, the idea that the world will get better, Abraham's actual experience was sometimes better and often worse. The immigrant experience of crossing borders and entering strange lands, as Abraham would have done on his pilgrimage, shapes the mind as it toughens the body and tightens the will.

The descendants of Abraham, heirs of the promise the guiding spirit made their ancestor, fared little better. They migrated to Egypt and became slaves. They followed the leadership of Moses and unexplainably escaped through the sea. It was an act of a terrifying mountain god who sent plagues. And even though Israel had its origins in Canaan, they were joined there by these Hebrews, the immigrant "hibiru" who "crossed over" the sea from Egypt. This pilgrim tribe contributed their story of Exodus from Egypt and shaped the people Israel would become. They brought their story of the liberator god who delivered them from bondage. They brought the liberator's law, which had been given to them on his thundering mountain. Their theology was branded into their experience toughened hides.

Overtime Israel gained a homeland until one day it was violently taken from them. The powerful Persian empire conquered the Jewish homeland and the Jews were taken away to Babylon in chains. Again on the sojourners trail, the exile from their homeland contributed to their feelings about their guiding spirit.

Rather than answering their prayers for a return to their homeland. The guiding spirit of Israel inspires them to bless the city they now inhabit. Reminiscent of his agreement with Abraham, they are to focus on their goals not their conditions. They are to bless these families on their way to the ends of the Earth.

This is a paradigm shift.

They are to bless the city of their enemies. They are called upon to represent the guiding spirit there, in that place, in Babylon. They are to be his people in a strange land.

Theology, thinking about God, is an embodied exercise.

Much later, Jesus, Peter, and Paul, building on Abraham, Israel, and the Prophets, make the radical turn. They execute a new idea: All of the Earth, not just Israel, is the holy land and all peoples, not only Israel, belong to the guiding spirit.

They launched a new community that is designed to be a sign of this potential future. And their efforts cost them all their lives. The quest to become human is fraught with dangers. According to the scriptures, this new community of the spirit is, like the resurrection of Jesus, another God hack. It is a post-empire and post-nationstate identity. It is a post social-self identity for the humankind. And as it emerges we can expect that it will introduce new ways of thinking about God.

Today, our migration into virtual space, as we are embedded in the coming electric sea of streaming data, our merging of the organic with the synthetic and the electronic (the orgathetic), our self-guided DIY evolution, our coming attempts to upload the human mind into a body of silicon, and our colonization of space all combine to create a new matrix within which to think about God. Perhaps we will even one day become hackers of the universe.

As the world changes rapidly around us, our guiding spirit calls for us to remember the things that God has done among us. But he isn't much for repetition. When he whispers again, he will breathe something new. He will breathe fire.

Postscript: The After Party

When I was a young boy, my grandfather told me he would live until the year 2000. This was decades before the millennial transition meant anything to anybody. The year 2000 seemed far away (and it was). In many ways, the year 2000 functioned as the ultimate symbol for the future. For some, the future was dark and foreboding, a dystopia. For my grandfather, the future was filled with positive possibilities. Perhaps, after centuries of war, we would know better. Scientific advancement and technological progress might save humankind from hunger, thirst, suffering, and death.

This, like many of our conversations, took place on the walkway between the living room and the dining room of our home. Like many houses in Latin America, our home on Calle San Salvador had high walls on all sides. Only the front of our home had windows, which allowed us to look across our street to a playground.

Inside the high walls of our home was an open-air garden with a small but fruitful banana tree and a pomegranate tree in the middle. The dining area was set at the back of the house behind this atrium, and the living area was set toward the front of the house. These two rooms were connected by an indoor walkway. The entrance to the cooking area opened along this walkway just a few feet from the dining area. All kinds of wonders emerged from there—corn tamales, sweet plantains with black beans, and chicken and rice.

My brother and I enjoyed sitting on the short wall that separated the walkway from the open-air terrarium, and plucking out the juicy red seeds from a ripe pomegranate. It seemed the hub of activity as it lay near the kitchen between the dining area and the living area. Directly in front of us, on the exterior wall of the kitchen, my grandfather pinned a map of the world.

We sat there all the time. Weekends were best. The map of the world pinned on the wall in front of us always led to interesting conversation. My grandfather loved history, politics, geography, and geology. He loved the idea of continental drift. The theory of continental drift emerged in the first two decades of the 1900s and must have been a hot topic when he was young. We talked about scientific discovery, political revolution, and the original position of all the continents before they began to drift—the super-continent known as Pangaea. As we sat there, he told us about the world, and we talked about any subject that might come up.

"Why will you live until the year 2000?" I asked.

"Because in the year 2000, there will be dancing in the streets," he said.

When my grandfather spoke those words—"There will be dancing in the streets"—vivid images of happiness erupted in my mind. For me, his words became words about The Future and not about any particular year in the future.

When the turn of the millennia finally arrived, there was indeed a spectacular day of dancing and celebration around the world. This experience brought his words to the front and center of my memory. (And, yes, he did live to see it).

Thanks to Abraham, we count the passing of the seconds, minutes, hours, days, and years. Could it be that these temporal markers are signs pointing to the end of all things, to the end of history and humanity, nature and eternity, and that the end to which it points is dancing?

The Christian scriptures indicate that God is making the world right through Jesus Christ. Images of this future in the Bible include a banquet to which everyone is welcomed. Predators will graze with their prey in God's future. Even technology will become a tool that makes the universe human: Weapons will be converted into instruments of agriculture. When God makes the world right, the purpose of history will be fulfilled, and God and humankind will be friends again.

This "right-making" of our world will no longer be a myth but an event. The world that God is making will eventually (or quite suddenly) consume the world in which we live. The call of Abraham, the exodus from Egypt, the crucifixion and resurrection of Jesus will have reached their end. God's redemptive struggle will be complete, and the Earth will end and begin again with dancing.

Some of us speak of this future as the Eschaton, that final "singularity" when "time is no more," the lordship of Jesus Christ is known to all, and questions about absolute truth are settled for everyone. The focus of this view is not particular events but the ultimate intentions of God. God has a point of view and a say in what the future will be like. Like humans, He can also create the future. This is the Future with a capital "F." When we complete our long walk to the end of the universe, it's his future that we will see.

Futurity - The Alternative Futures

We moved to Miami when I was still young. The tensions between the United States and the Soviet Union were high in those days. That's how much the world can change in a relatively short period of time: The Soviet Union doesn't even exist today. But in those days, the world stood anxiously at the threshold of nuclear war.

Even in elementary school, we were all quite aware that the world could go in at least a couple of ways. We were reminded of this when we did the "what to do in case of nuclear attack" drill. They didn't call it this, but second graders aren't stupid. The alarms rang, and we got away from the windows and hid under our little desks.

The future wasn't a predetermined event. It wasn't closed. The future was open. It wasn't our decision to make, but somebody somewhere was in a position to choose one future over another. In other words, we knew the future was not static, but dynamic. The future waited for decisions to be made and actions to be taken in the present. The decisions of some of us had the power to affect all of us.

So there were at least two possible futures. That's why when I speak of the future I really mean the *futures*, plural. At any given point in our personal lives and in our communal lives, many futures are possible. We have some say in shaping the future. Of course, many factors—societal, technological, economic, environmental, geological, political, and the like—are beyond our control. But many of us feel that we have, to a greater or lesser degree, some say about our tomorrow.

This is the future with a lowercase f. We have power to shape the present because the future is open, dynamic, and plural. We can make big changes or little changes. Some of us can influence tomorrow more than others. The future is not egalitarian. It plays favorites. But to some extent each of us has a say in the trajectory of our tomorrows. These are the alternative futures.

The Fourth Move

When I lived in New Orleans one of my favorite religion professors, Fisher Humphreys, told a story to explain his understanding of what happened when Jesus died. The story went something like this.

Dr. Humphreys was playing in a chess tournament in the UK. One of his matches ended in a defeat in 11 moves. His opponent leaned over and said to him, "You lost that game on your fourth move."

Dr. Humphreys wanted a more literal interpretation of the match. "No, I lost on the eleventh move," he replied.

His opponent offered to show him where the game went wrong, and sure enough Dr. Humphreys was able to see that on his fourth move, his defeat was inevitable and his opponent's victory was imminent. He may have delayed defeat a move or two, but eventually defeat would come.

Then Dr. Humphreys connected this story to our conversation about the death of Christ. The cross, he said, was the enemy's fourth move.

That has a lot to do with the future. We live in the space between the brutal experience of the cross and the wondrous whispers of the resurrection.

A human future is possible because God is calling us towards it. Like a chess match, any creature, human or otherwise, that oppose God's activity to make the world human are free to move their pieces in any way they please. They may create alternate futures and formations that they hope will prevent a world made human.

But God has set out to create the world we cannot create without him. And he is doing so among us and with us. That is the gospel: God is making the world human and he is doing this through the man Jesus Christ who was crucified for our sins according to the scriptures and who was raised from the dead by the power of God.

The cross was our fourth move. The resurrection was His response.

My grandfather envisioned a future with dancing. The scriptures do too... a future of dancing and dining in the Kingdom of God, a future at a party thrown by the Source of all life and joy. That's the "capital F" future, the eschatological future, the future that gives everything meaning.

In the meantime, we are the ones who have to work this future out so that traces of it can leap to life in the present and in the futures we create. We must make the dream and the deed coincide.

The Glory Road

"Men wanted for hazardous journey. Small wages, bitter cold, long months of complete darkness, constant danger, safe return doubtful. Honor and recognition in case of success."

While no documented evidence exists, this advertising text is widely attributed to Ernest Shackleton, the adventurer who sought to cross Antarctica in 1914. Shackleton is believed to have run the ad in London newspapers in order to assemble a crew. His attempt to cross the frozen continent is one of the greatest feats of leadership of all time.

While most of us would never have responded to Shackleton's ad, many of us understand the impulse and why it drew such a crowd of applicants.

It was that same impulse that calls some of us to dedicate their lives to the space program. One of my favorite places on Earth is the Kennedy Space Center. And my favorite spot in the Space Center is the memorial commemorating the women and men who've lost their lives in service to the program. The memorial is a huge wall divided into multiple squares. The names of those who gave their lives cover only a small portion of the surface. The most striking feature of this memorial is all the empty spaces, the ones waiting to be filled.

Our mission in the universe is not only to confront and subdue evil in the name of Jesus, it is also to reach out and touch the stars. Our purpose is not only to cast out the spirit of xenophobia, it is to explore the full magnificence of life.

I looked at the memorial and focused on the names of a particular crew. On January 28, 1986, I'd stood outside downtown Orlando and watched the takeoff of the space shuttle Challenger. That mission was special. Christa McAuliffe, the schoolteacher from New Hampshire and the first private citizen to travel into space, was on board.

The future imagined by science fiction writers was coming to pass before our very eyes. We were going into space. Not just the aviators, not just the elite troop of men who paved the way into outer space, but the average citizen: a teacher. It seemed only a matter of time before every earthling would be a "citizen of the galaxy."

As I stood there watching the impossible become reality, the column of smoke on which the small manned shuttlecraft rode split in two. I'd seen launches before. This was something new.

At first, I didn't understand what the sky was telling me. Only slowly, as the smoke spread, and then began to trail back to Earth, did the meaning open in my mind. I was watching something that would be long remembered. I was experiencing in that moment every risk taken and every self-sacrifice made from the time we took the first steps out of Africa until now as we continue to take strides to colonize space.

I couldn't stop staring into the sky as the streaks of white smoke marked the canvas of blue. I watched silently as the Challenger fragmented into pieces and fell through the air into the sea. As though gazing at a celestial Rorschach inkblot, some saw a needless tragedy. Why can't humans just be content with staying here on Earth? Others looked at it and saw the portrait of every person who refuses to stay safely at home and leave great questions unanswered.

The history of exploration is marked by tragedy. Still, we explore. Our deep compulsion to explain who and what we are will drive us. We will explore the most distant points in space, probe the deepest oceans, map the mind, tinker with the human genome, and scan every other arena of curiosity. We will turn over every microcellular rock in search of the meaning of the universe. We will search the heavens for another Earth, for signs of life among the stars. And, all along, what we are really seeking is the meaning of being us.

Images of the Future

Our images of the future shape us. I see a future with dancing. I see a future in which humankind steps up to its responsibility and becomes the guardian of all creation. Relationships with others of all races will be characterized by the love one has for a brother and sister. This future is not one we will create on our own. It will be given to us as a gift, as we work hard to enter into it.

To get there will need to twist our heads around towards love. We will need our imaginations opened to new possibilities for the human story, the vanguard of which is the Jesus story.

Some among us will embrace the open, dynamic, plural futures as responsibility, and embrace our ability to make choices in the present.

At the personal level there is no guarantee of success. All we can be sure of is an opportunity to discover a little of what we are called to become, or perhaps to inch humanity forward. Sometimes, however, we will feel powerless before the immense mechanisms that keep the world turning. We can rage against the machine, but it doesn't hear us. Blame the politicians. Blame the church. Blame God. Sometimes it feels as though there's nothing we can do. Big problems seem to demand big solutions. But big solutions are not the same as monolithic solutions or flashy solutions.

In much of contemporary human culture, "success" has become a synonym for "celebrity." Even in the Church we exalt celebrity-ism. But deep inside we know this isn't how the world becomes human.

This week I received an email from someone in Africa. He told the story of a very elderly woman who lives in a remote village miles from the nearest city. As a young girl, she had been forced to serve the Portuguese as a slave. She experienced ten years of colonial war and eighteen years of civil war. Her exposure to Whites had generally been an experience of harshness and brutality. Two White men had now come to visit her village. In her culture, the women wash the hands of guests before and after meals. At first, she looked with suspicion at these two White men who had traveled to her remote region of Africa. Then the White men washed her hands. They asked for forgiveness for the past. As they day came to a close, she called her grandchildren over to her and told them with joy, "My hands were washed by two White men today."

I can only imagine that the look on her face revealed the meaning of history. The world was finally becoming human around her, and she had lived long enough to see it.

We are not called to celebrity. We are called to something far greater. Like these two men in a remote corner of Africa, we are called to make fire.

Ironically, the fear of feeling insignificant can keep us from taking our place in the noble cause of making the universe human. Even the smallest actions, such as humbling yourself and washing someone's hands, can be heroic. Celebrity is nothing when compared to what it means to be a human connected to community and purpose.

The future is open, dynamic, and plural. A detailed map of the future cannot be created. But we can see our world through the story of Jesus and look at the direction God is going. I want to summon the spirit of adventure in us all because there is something so deeply right with our world, something so deeply worth experiencing, something worth saving. This is the epic journey of discovery to which God calls us by his spirit.

If Jesus could run an ad like Shackleton's today, perhaps it would say something like this:

Heroes Wanted

for an epic quest to hack the universe.

Starting with Earth.

Safe return doubtful.

SHE

hackers of the universe

An unspecified date in the future

The agenda was packed with the expected items: the use of robots in war, the deployment of gynoids to populate red-light districts, to allow or to fight the biopunk underground and their out-of-control race for genetic enhancements, the Eight Planet Project, which might be the tipping point to colonization of the solar system beyond the modest colonies on Luna and Mars. Those were the expected issues, and the panel, as usual, would be divided over them.

But the final item on the agenda was the Human Project. The implications of this project reached so far and wide that it would not bring division, only silence, to the room. The developments in the Human Project were so far beyond anything else humankind had ever achieved that they didn't even have the right words to discuss the implications.

She rose slowly to her feet. As she did so her chair disassembled into a swarm of millions of tiny components and, to the naked organic eye, disappeared. The swarm would follow her, invisibly, silently, until needed to reassemble as a lectern or a love seat, a segway or an exoskeleton.

She knew, as she prepared to address the panel, that this moment could define human destiny forever. Whatever words she spoke at this moment, as chair of the multi-planetary panel on the human future, could set them on a path so radically different that future and past generations would not be able to recognize the worlds in which the other lived. Indeed, they would not even be able to recognize each other.

She accessed an info stream through a nano-wave network port embedded in her genetically-enhanced brain which allowed her to review, in just a few seconds, the major breakthroughs in human history beginning with the discovery of fire to the latest models of bending time and space.

She smiled at the hubris of the early 21st century, how they believed they knew so much. They thought that huge changes were right upon them. They were wrong on two counts. The major disruptions came much later than they expected. And the changes they had imagined were minuscule compared to the ones that actually came. *What we know can be placed in three categories,* she thought. *There's what we know we know. There's what we know that we don't know. And there's what we don't know that we don't know.* The "unknown unknowns" had proven to be a major force in shaping futurity.

As she rose to her feet she had a strange sensation, as if she had done this a million times throughout the aeons. All of her life she had been visited by a recurring vision: an animal skull turned upside down with a blazing fire burning within it.

The world of that vision was a world unlike any she had ever seen or experienced before, not even on her trips to Earth. Her vision was teeming with life, bursting at the seams with biotic energy, exploding with diversity and possibilities. Sometimes the visions were so real that she would squeeze shut her orgathetic eyes and open them just to see if it was really there.

The vision opened before her again now and, as she looked around the table at the other members of the panel, she wondered what, if anything, the vision was trying to say to her.

MORE FROM THE INTERNATIONAL MENTORING NETWORK

For more information about the International Mentoring Network, visit our main site at http://theimn.com. (Be sure to subscribe to our newsletter!) Follow the IMN on twitter at @theimn.

To follow Alex McManus, check out his website at alexmcmanus.org, twitter at @alex_mcmanus, Instagram at http://instagram.com/xandermcmanus, Facebook at https://www.facebook.com/alexmcmanus .

ADDITIONAL TRAINING AND RESOURCES
The IMN offers training for leaders interested in developing their strategic foresight, creativity, and spiritual leadership. See our website for more information - http://theimn.com

A Personal Note:

Thanks for reading my first book, Makers of Fire. As an independent writer, I depend on you to recommend my work to others. Your help in spreading the word through social media and personal referrals is greatly appreciated. -Alex